AMERICA LOVES®
HAMBURGER

AMERICA LOVES®

HAMBURGER

101 All-Time Best Recipes

LINDA WEST ECKHARDT

Illustrated by Lauren Jarrett

WINGS BOOKS
New York • Avenel, New Jersey

This 1994 edition is published by Wings Books,
distributed by Random House Value Publishing, Inc.,
40 Engelhard Avenue, Avenel, New Jersey 07001,
by arrangement with GuildAmerica Books®/Doubleday Book & Music
Clubs, Inc.

GuildAmerica Books®, and America Loves® are registered trademarks of
Doubleday Book & Music Clubs, Inc.

America Loves® Hamburger was prepared and produced by Michael
Friedman Publishing Group, Inc.

Random House
New York • Toronto • London • Sydney • Auckland

Illustrator: Lauren Jarrett

Printed and bound in the United States of America

Library of Congress Cataloging-in-Publication Data

Eckhardt, Linda West, 1939-
    America loves hamburger : 101 all-time best recipes / Linda West
Eckhardt ; illustrated by Lauren Jarret.
        p.   cm.
    Includes index.
    ISBN 0-517-11843-2
    1. Cookery (Beef) 2. Hamburgers. 3. Meat loaf. 4. Meatballs.
I. Title
TX749.5.B43E33   1994
641.6'62--dc20   94-11873
                                                          CIP

8 7 6 5 4 3 2

Thanks to the National Beef Council and the Texas Beef
Industry Council for their generous support and
valuable information. Thanks also to Marian Tripp
for aiding in the research of this book.

This book is dedicated to

Bettie Henry,

a fine cook and home economist who can serve two
people or two thousand with equal aplomb.
Thanks Bettie, for your continuing support.

CONTENTS

INTRODUCTION

As American as apple pie, as dear to our hearts as the flag, hamburgers are the quintessential American dish. This is one subject about which everyone has an opinion. You may like your hamburger grilled with catsup and pickles. I like mine on a sesame seed bun with mayo, lettuce, and tomatoes. My husband wants his in a weekly meatloaf.

But one thing's for sure, it's positively un-American not to like hamburger. And regardless of the latest wave of guilt about fats, almost everybody I know will sneak off for a good juicy burger once in awhile. In fact, 44 percent of all the meat meals eaten in the United States are still centered around hamburger.

When I got to thinking about hamburger and the place it has in American cuisine, real American cuisine, I started thumbing through my flour-splattered recipe box and digging out all my old favorites. Then I asked around and discovered that my friends—no matter how avant-garde—got this positively fond look on their faces when I asked them if they had a favorite hamburger recipe.

Hunt that favorite recipe up, I told them; I want to put all our good recipes in one place—say in a book—so we can find them, so they won't get lost.

Recipes began falling on me like the proverbial pennies from heaven. I discovered some fascinating regional differences. What my Minneapolis pal likes varies markedly from what my Miami buddy cooks. Whether a cook likes to add a Tex-Mex twist, a Caribbean wrinkle, or a California spin to the recipe may depend on

where they went for their best vacation, where he was stationed in the army, or where she lived while she went to college.

It turns out that Americans like ground beef not only in hamburgers of infinite permutation, but also in meatloaves, casseroles, stir-fries, microwave dishes, chilies, soups, and stews. I got recipes for ground beef pâtés and sausages. I found excellent recipes for low-fat, low-cholesterol entrées. Hamburger even turns up in salads and appetizers.

It seems that the one food that binds the people of this country is hamburger meat. We eat it everywhere—from Puerto Rico to Alaska, from Portland, Maine, to Portland, Oregon. We eat it any way, from hamburgers and meatloaves to countless middle-of-the-plate preparations. You'll find hamburger on the menu in one guise or another in restaurants from the local bar and grill all the way to the toniest haute cuisine haunt. Let's face it. We Americans love hamburger.

We've tested the recipes in this book using various ground meat products and believe we've recommended the most ideal ground meat for each dish. In some recipes you'll see a combination of ground beef with veal, turkey, or pork. These recipes can always be made with just one ground meat, usually beef, but you'll get the best results by mixing the meats.

What's great about cooking ground meat is it's easy, it's fast, and it's fun. There are no long, complicated procedures. There isn't a sinkful of dirty dishes at the end of dinner. There is no interminable wait while supper cooks. Ground meat dinners are quick, satisfying, and simple.

These recipes reflect the country's growing awareness about fats and cholesterol. We offer a nutritional analysis with each recipe. We used the USDA's nutritional data in a computer-generated program. I tested all recipes at home using 15-percent fat lean hamburger meat. The nutritional analyses shown at the bottom of each recipe are based on this low-fat product. If you use 30-percent fat hamburger, the fat and cholesterol numbers will zoom.

Cooks may be puzzled about how best to cook with the new lower-fat hamburger. This cookbook will show you how. The recipes collected here reflect several trends:

• The reality of the new ground beef products available to most Americans.

• The wish of American cooks and diners to have healthy, brightly flavored dishes that can be prepared quickly and easily.

• A reflection of the growing sophistication among cooks and the willingness to try new combinations.

America Loves Hamburger offers good hearty food that will satisfy a family and improve its health at the same time. The recipes offered are not only simple, quick to prepare, and tantalizing, they are also abundant in flavor, texture, color, and nutrition. Enjoy.

WHERE'S THE BEEF?

Not so long ago, hamburger was hamburger. And it was usually less than a dollar a pound. But then we began to worry about fats and cholesterol, and before you knew it we had a dizzying array of choices under the heading "ground beef."

If you read the fine print on labels today, you're likely to see fat contents ranging from 30 percent for old-fashioned regular ground beef down to a mere 4 percent and prices that range all over the map.

So what's the best buy? I bought a pound each of several different ground beef products. At home, I weighed them into equal 4-ounce patties, peppered them, then broiled them on a rack, about 4 minutes on each side.

I was trying to see how much fat and moisture dripped out, what each hamburger weighed when it was cooked, how it tasted, and how much it cost— per bite. There was almost no difference in taste or moisture-fat loss between the 22-percent and 16-percent fat hamburgers.

Drop the fat content to 10 percent or to 4 percent and the hamburger got a little dicey. Dense, gray, and solid as a pat of wet cement, the lowest-fat product seemed to need the most seasoning, and it certainly cost the most.

Healthy Choice is a Con-Agra reconstituted ground beef product that contains a solution of beef stock, Oatrim™, water, and encapsulated salt. The raw product contains only 4 percent fat, yet derives 28 percent of its calories from fat. As far as I'm concerned, it's too processed and too pricey.

That poor 30-percent-fat burger shrank nearly by half and didn't seem to me to be a bargain in either the health department or at the bank.

For my money, I'm sticking to mid-range ground beef products. I like the taste. They don't cost too much. And I can—to use the old-fashioned/newly stylish term—stretch them with ground beef dishes containing various complex carbohydrates for interesting new tastes.

COMPARISONS OF GROUND BEEF PRODUCTS

	Fat Content	Price per lb.	Weight After Cooking (4-oz. raw patty)
Healthy Choice extra-lean ground beef	4%	$2.99	3.2 oz.
Leanest ground beef	10%	2.28	3.1
Extra-lean ground beef	15%	1.98	3.0
Lean ground beef	22%	1.78	2.9
Regular ground beef	30%	1.19	2.3

SAFETY FIRST

Is hamburger safe to feed your family? Yes, provided you cook it thoroughly. And you don't have to be a lab technician to tell. Eat only hamburger that has been cooked until it no longer shows any pink color and has juices that run clear without any pinkish tinge.

Cordelia Morris, public affairs specialist for the Food Safety and Inspection Service says, "all products of animal nature carry bacteria and [only] thorough cooking kills that bacteria."

It is important to remember that freezing does not kill bacteria. And that meat products should always be kept below 40°F or above 140°F. The 100-degree range between these two temperatures is ideal for the growth and multiplication of microbes.

Harmful bacteria, including *E. coli*, are carried in the guts of animals and can contaminate the meat during the butchering process. Your best assumption is that all meats carry some harmful bacteria. But these bacteria are real wimps in the face of heat. Your best defense is thorough cooking.

If you're eating out and the waiter inquires as to how you'd like your meat cooked, reply "cooked through." Ground meats are particularly risky because harmful bacteria can be found throughout the meat, whereas on steaks or roasts those bacteria are on the surface and are more likely to be killed by the hot grill or a blast of hot air from the oven.

All ground meat should be cooked to an internal temperature of 155°F.

In a nutshell, here's your best defense against *E. coli,* salmonella, campylobacter, and other harmful bacteria found in meats, according to the U.S. Department of Agriculture:

- After shopping, quickly refrigerate or freeze meats.
- Use refrigerated ground meat within three days, frozen products within three to four months.
- Wash your hands, utensils, and work areas with hot, soapy water after contact with raw meat.
- Wash your hands after using the bathroom or diapering an infant (remember we're animals, too, and we can pass along harmful bacteria to each other).
- Cook meat until it's gray or brown. Juices should run clear with no trace of pink. This is true for all meat, poultry, and fish.
- In a restaurant, send back any meat, poultry, or fish product that does not appear to be thoroughly cooked.
- When barbecuing or grilling, never put cooked hamburgers or other meats back on the same platter you used when they were raw.
- Never cut vegetables on the same cutting board or with the same knife you used to prepare raw meat unless you've thoroughly washed the board or knife with hot, soapy water.
- Microwave carefully. If your oven is a lower wattage than that shown in the cooking instructions, you'll need to cook food longer or at a higher setting.
- For more information call the U.S. Department of Agriculture hotline at 1-800-535-4555. Home economists and registered dietitians answer questions daily.

Chapter One

THE TOP TWENTY HAMBURGERS

You'll get fierce arguments from people about just what the "All-American" hamburger is. To those from the Midwest, it's likely to be some incarnation of the famous White Castle burger: small, square, and greasy. To the New Yorker, it's likely to be a simple grilled thick patty of meat with catsup and a bun.

In the panhandle of Texas, where I grew up, the hamburger of my youth was a grilled thin patty of meat on a bun with mustard and mayo, finely shredded iceberg lettuce, thin slices of tomato and onion, and "hamburger" pickles, which were either sour or dill. We bought these hamburgers at a drive-in where carhops brought food and snappy replies to the raw-as-hamburger teenagers who filled up the place. We listened to Elvis on the radio and cruised Main Street. We ate french fries drowned in catsup and drank Cokes by the gallon. My entire adolescence reeks of greasy yellow paper wadded up around the big-as-a-dinner-plate hamburgers they sold at the Double K Drive-In.

My cousin Kaki Thurber, who came along five years after me, chased her hamburger down with Tater Tots, the latest invention. She recalls the twang of

Patsy Cline on the radio and the aroma of the feed lots that circled our hometown of Hereford. We were, you see, vividly there at both ends of the food chain, inhaling the aroma from beginning to end.

My friend Peggy, as a teenager, worked in a resort on Mackinac Island, Michigan, where the favorite was something called a Wimpy Burger. In that incarnation the hamburger was thick, hot, and dressed with chopped green olives and lots of mayonnaise.

I'm told that in certain parts of the country, only Miracle Whip salad dressing will make a *true* hamburger.

The classic American hamburger, by my lights, is revered for its simplicity. The meat is not fancied up with fillings. The bun is a plain hamburger bun. The tomato can be as pale pink as the inside of a seashell and just as tasteless. The lettuce can be as white as Belgian endive, but it must be iceberg. It's what I call America.

Wimpy Burgers

Popeye may have gained strength from spinach, but Wimpy knew what was good for you. Old-fashioned hamburgers with a Wimpy twist—chopped green olives and shredded lettuce. Popular on Michigan's Mackinac Island, these burgers are still a hit at a backyard party.

makes 4 servings

1   pound lean ground beef
1   small onion, minced
2   cloves garlic, pressed
     salt and freshly ground black pepper to taste
4   whole wheat hamburger buns
4   tablespoons mayonnaise
½   cup shredded iceberg lettuce
¼   cup chopped green olives

Mix together the beef, onions, and garlic. Season with salt and pepper, then form into 4 equal-sized patties. Cover with waxed paper and refrigerate until you've preheated the grill.

Lay a charcoal fire in the grill, and once the coals are glowing white and red, grill the burgers about 2 inches from the fire, until done, about 4 minutes per side.

Once you've turned the burgers, lay the buns on top of the cooked side to heat through. Spread buns with mayo, divide lettuce and olives among them, and top each with a smoking hot burger. Serve with potato chips and old-fashioned Cokes for an all-American backyard classic.

Per serving: 453 calories, 35 g. fat, 108 mg. cholesterol, 588 mg. sodium

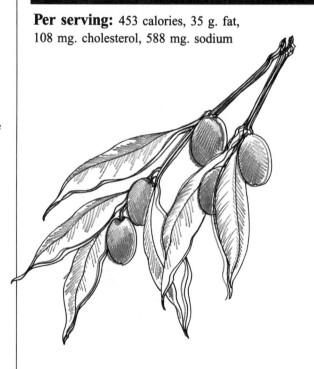

Cut-the-Fat Burger

If you're missing hamburgers because you think they're too fatty, but you hate burgers made with ground turkey because it's too dry, try a combination for a much lighter, yet full-flavored burger. Serve on toasted fat-free French bread spread with mustard and heaps of lettuce, tomatoes, pickles, and onions. You may not miss the fat at all.

makes 6 servings

1	**green onion, including top, minced**
1	**pound ground turkey**
½	**pound lean ground beef**
½	**cup soft whole wheat bread crumbs**
¼	**cup barbecue sauce**
	salt and freshly ground black pepper to taste
	toasted French bread
	mustard
	lettuce
	tomatoes

Combine onions, ground meats, bread crumbs, barbecue sauce, salt, and pepper. Squish the mixture together with your hands, then form into 6 equal patties, each about ¾ inch thick. Cover and refrigerate.

Preheat a charcoal or gas grill. Flip the hamburger patties onto the hot grill and cook about 5 minutes on each side, turning once.

Serve on toasted French bread with mustard, lettuce, and tomatoes, and pickles to accompany.

Per serving: 267 calories, 11 g. fat, 103 mg. cholesterol, 711 mg. sodium

Caribbean Burgers

Garnish with a wedge of mango and a sliver of lime.

makes 6 servings

Burgers:
1½   **pounds lean ground beef**
6   **whole wheat sesame seed buns**
    cracked pepper and salt to taste

Caribbean Sauce:
1   **tablespoon olive oil**
6   **cloves garlic, chopped**
1   **large yellow onion, diced**
1   **large green bell pepper, seeded and diced**
1   **cup pimiento-stuffed green olives, chopped**
1   **can (16 ounces) tomatoes (with juice)**
2   **teaspoons fresh oregano leaves, or 1 teaspoon dried**
1   **teaspoon fresh tarragon leaves, or ½ teaspoon dried**
1   **teaspoon fresh basil leaves, or ½ teaspoon dried**
1   **tablespoon fresh lemon juice**
¼   **cup fresh cilantro leaves**
    salt and pepper to taste

Divide meat into 6 thick patties. Season with pepper and salt. Cover and refrigerate; preheat grill.

Meanwhile, in a medium saucepan over medium-high heat, make the sauce. Sauté in oil the garlic, onions, peppers, and olives until the onions are beginning to brown on the edges. Then add tomatoes and juice, oregano, tarragon, and basil leaves. Stir in lemon juice and simmer 15 to 20 minutes. The sauce should be thick and rich. Toss in cilantro leaves, taste, and adjust seasonings with salt and pepper.

Grill the meat patties until cooked through over the charcoal grill. After you've turned the meat the first time, heat the buns by placing the split and stacked buns on top of the cooking meat patties.

To serve, place a patty on the split hot bun, add a generous serving of cooked sauce, and serve on a plate with a knife and fork.

Per serving: 388 calories, 28 g. fat, 106 mg. cholesterol, 850 mg. sodium

Maize Burgers

The crunch of corn, topped with your favorite salsa, makes a southwestern hamburger that is delicious served on a flour tortilla along with shredded iceberg lettuce and lime wedges.

makes 4 servings

1	**pound lean ground beef**
¾	**cup yellow cornmeal**
1	**tablespoon lime juice**
1	**large egg white, whisked until frothy**
1	**teaspoon cumin (or to taste)**
2	**teaspoons chili powder**
	salt and freshly ground black pepper to taste
1	**jalapeño (or to taste), seeded and finely chopped**
1	**tablespoon vegetable oil**
1	**cup corn kernels, cut from the cob, frozen, or canned and drained**
1	**cup fresh salsa**
4	**flour tortillas**

Combine the beef, cornmeal, lime juice, egg white, cumin, chili powder, salt, pepper, and jalapeño. Mix together lightly. Shape into 4 patties and reserve on a sheet of waxed paper.

Over medium-high heat, heat a 12-inch skillet, then add the oil to coat the bottom. Place patties in the skillet and cook, turning once, until cooked through and deep golden brown, about 3 to 5 minutes on each side.

Meanwhile, in a small saucepan, combine corn and salsa and heat. Heat tortillas wrapped in a cloth, or on paper plates, in the microwave, 15 seconds at 100 percent (HIGH).

To serve, place a cooked patty on a flour tortilla, top with a serving of salsa, and fold. Add shredded lettuce, if desired.

Per serving: 486 calories, 24 g. fat, 160 mg. cholesterol, 836 mg. sodium

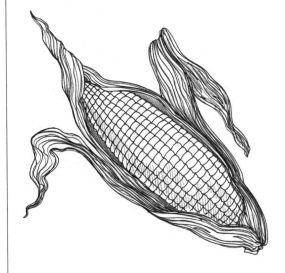

Pine Nut Burgers

For these Italian-style hamburgers, shape them like rockets, then serve in hard rolls along with red-tipped lettuce, ripe red tomatoes, and basil leaves.

makes 6 servings

1½	pounds lean ground beef
1	medium onion, finely chopped
2	large cloves garlic, finely chopped
1	cup dry bread crumbs
½	cup Parmesan or Romano cheese
¼	cup pine nuts
½	cup finely chopped fresh parsley
2	large eggs
	salt and freshly ground black pepper to taste
6	hard rolls
	olive oil
	frilly lettuce
	thick tomato slices

Mix ground beef with onions, garlic, bread crumbs, cheese, pine nuts, parsley, eggs, salt, and pepper. Form into 6 equal-sized rocket-shaped patties, about 1½ inches thick and 5 inches long.

Pan-broil in a hot, dry skillet, until browned and crisp, about 5 minutes on each side.

Wipe rolls with oil, then tuck in burgers, lettuce, and tomatoes. Garnish with whole basil leaves.

Per serving: 528 calories, 26 g. fat, 199 mg. cholesterol, 1,289 mg. sodium

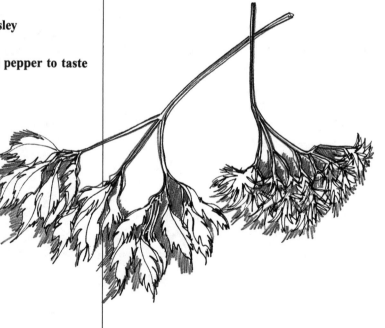

Basil Beef Pockets

Here are hamburgers in pita pockets, flavored with the Italian taste of fresh basil, tomatoes, and ruffled red-tipped lettuce leaves.

makes 4 servings

1	**pound lean ground beef**
¼	**cup reduced-sodium soy sauce**
2	**tablespoons red wine vinegar**
2	**tablespoons fresh basil leaves, minced**
4	**cloves garlic, minced**
3	**tablespoons olive oil**
1	**large carrot, thinly sliced**
1	**yellow bell pepper, seeded and thinly sliced**
1	**cup broccoli florets**
1	**cup button mushrooms, sliced**
1	**medium purple onion, thinly sliced**
¼	**cup water**
2	**teaspoons cornstarch**
2	**plum tomatoes, finely chopped**
4	**warmed pita pockets, halved**
	red-tipped lettuce leaves
	basil sprigs

Divide ground beef into 4 equal-sized pieces and form into patties. Place in a glass dish.

Whisk together soy sauce, vinegar, minced basil, garlic, and 1 tablespoon oil. Pour over the beef patties, cover, and refrigerate.

Meanwhile, heat remaining 2 tablespoons oil in a wok over high heat and stir-fry one item at a time—the carrots, peppers, broccoli, mushrooms, and onions—until crisp-tender and beginning to brown, about 3 to 5 minutes. Remove the vegetables to a bowl and keep warm.

Combine water, cornstarch, and marinade. Place in the wok and heat until bubbly and thick. Add all the vegetables and beef patties to the wok and cook through. Add tomatoes.

To serve, line the pita pockets with lettuce, then place a patty and a serving of vegetables in each pocket. Garnish with basil sprigs and serve at once.

Per serving: 477 calories, 30 g. fat, 92 mg. cholesterol, 997 mg. sodium

Hamburgers With Cracked Black Pepper and Mango Chutney

Serve these hamburgers in pita pockets in a nest of butterhead lettuce.

makes 6 servings

1½	pounds lean ground beef
¼	cup sherry or cognac (optional)
8	tablespoons cracked black pepper
1½	cups mango chutney
6	pita pockets, sliced open butterhead lettuce leaves

Form ground beef into 6 equal-sized patties. Cook in hot buttered sauté pan until brown on the outside but still rare in the middle.

Remove the cooked meat and keep warm. Deglaze the sauté pan by pouring sherry or cognac, if desired, or a couple tablespoons of water in the pan and boiling it almost away, scraping the bottom of the skillet. Add chutney and cracked pepper and heat. Nestle the meat patties atop the chutney and heat through.

Line each pita with lettuce. Insert a meat patty with chutney sauce, and serve.

Per serving: 554 calories, 23 g. fat, 102 mg. cholesterol, 156 mg. sodium

Teriyaki Burgers

Serve these sweet, smoky, grilled burgers on hot hamburger buns with slices of purple onion and red-tipped lettuce.

makes 6 servings

½	cup bottled teriyaki sauce
2	tablespoons minced onions
2	slices of bread
2	pounds lean ground beef
2	egg whites
6	hamburger buns

Preheat outdoor grill or the broiler. Combine ¼ cup teriyaki sauce with the onions. Let it stand 5 minutes.

Tear bread into bite-sized pieces, then cover with a small amount of water. Let stand 5 minutes, then squeeze excess water out.

Add bread, ground beef, and egg whites to onion mixture, mixing well. Shape into 6 patties.

Cook patties until done, about 15 minutes, turning occasionally and brushing with remaining ¼ cup teriyaki sauce from time to time. Serve on buns.

Per serving: 470 calories, 31 g. fat, 228 mg. cholesterol, 985 mg. sodium

Quesadilla Burgers on Flour Tortillas

In a Mexican-style burger, the sauce's secret is a pinch of curry powder. No one will ever guess!

makes 6 servings

Burgers:

1½	**pounds lean ground beef**
	cracked black pepper and salt
6	**large flour tortillas**
1	**cup grated white cheese (Monterey Jack or Mexican white)**

Quesadilla Sauce:

1	**tablespoon vegetable oil**
4	**cloves garlic, sliced**
1	**cup sliced mushrooms**
1	**cup yellow onion, cut into 1-inch squares**
1	**cup poblano chili peppers, seeded and cut into 1-inch squares**
	pinch of curry powder
1	**can (16 ounces) tomatoes (with juice)**
	salt and pepper to taste

Form ground beef into 6 equal patties. Season to taste with pepper and salt, cover, and set aside while you preheat a charcoal grill.

Separate the flour tortillas, grate the cheese, and set aside.

Meanwhile, make the sauce. Sauté in hot oil over medium-high the garlic, mushrooms, onions, and chilies until the onions begin to brown. Add curry powder and cook a minute more, then add tomatoes and juice and simmer for 15 to 20 minutes. The sauce should be thick and rich. Adjust seasonings to taste with salt and pepper.

Cook the patties over charcoal fire until done through, then place one cooked patty onto each flour tortilla, top with a generous dollop of white cheese, and slather on Quesadilla Sauce. Serve on a plate with a knife and fork.

Per serving: 622 calories, 35 g. fat, 128 mg. cholesterol, 670 mg. sodium

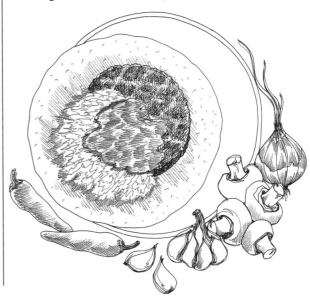

Blue Cheese Burgers

Cook these burgers over low heat so that the blue cheese won't melt through and be lost. Serve on English muffins with butterhead lettuce and Dijon mustard, and cornichons on the side.

makes 4 servings

1	**pound lean ground beef**
3	**ounces blue cheese, crumbled**
	freshly ground black pepper to taste
4	**English muffins**
2	**teaspoons Dijon mustard**
1	**medium purple onion, thinly sliced**
1	**medium tomato, thinly sliced**
4	**pieces butterhead lettuce, washed, dried, and torn into bite-sized pieces**

Crumble the ground beef with the blue cheese. Pepper generously, then squish together with your hands. Form into 4 thick patties. Cover and refrigerate while you prepare a charcoal fire or preheat your gas grill.

Meanwhile, prepare the muffins, condiments, and vegetables and place them near the barbecue. Grill the hamburgers, until cooked through, usually no more than 5 minutes on each side, taking care not to have the fire too hot.

To serve, smear the muffins with mustard and top with a cooked burger, purple onion, lettuce, and tomato.

Per serving: 448 calories, 26 g. fat, 108 mg. cholesterol, 589 mg. sodium

Balzar's Burgers

Al and Carol Balzar have made an art of using their gas grill for burgers. They use fruitwood chips in a pan to create smoke; they heat both burners of the gas grill, then turn off the left side and cook these burgers on the OFF side, with the lid closed. In this way, the good cheese does not melt through the burgers and fall out. The smoky flavor permeates the meat, and they've created a winning burger.

makes 4 servings

1¼	pounds lean ground beef
2	tablespoons fresh chopped basil
2	ounces brie cheese
1	ounce white cheddar cheese
1	small onion, chopped
1	teaspoon black pepper
1	clove garlic, pressed
4	large hamburger buns or Kaiser rolls
4	teaspoons mayonnaise
4	large leaves Romaine lettuce, torn
1	large tomato, thinly sliced

Crumble ground beef into a bowl, then mix in the basil, brie, cheddar, onions, pepper, and garlic, squishing it all together with your hands. Form into 4 thick patties, then refrigerate while you preheat the grill.

If you're using a gas grill, preheat both burners. If you're using charcoal, mound the charcoal into one spot and light it. When the charcoal is covered with a white ash, you're ready to cook.

Add a small pan of water-soaked fruitwood chips to the base of the grill. Place hamburgers over the hot part of the grill for about 45 seconds, just long enough to get the good grill marks on the meat, then remove the patties to a cooler part of the grill, cover, and cook until done through, about 10 minutes.

Meanwhile, prepare the buns by smearing on mayonnaise. A few moments before you're ready to serve, stack buns onto the meat patties to heat the buns through. Serve each patty on a bun along with lettuce and tomatoes.

Per serving: 536 calories, 34 g. fat, 133 mg. cholesterol, 298 mg. sodium

The All-American Hamburger

The classic American hamburger is revered for its simplicity. The meat is not fancied up with fillings. The bun is a plain hamburger bun. The tomato can be as pale pink as the inside of a seashell and just as tasteless. The lettuce can be as white as Belgian endive. It's what we like in America. Our home-grown, all-American best.

makes 8 servings

2	**pounds lean ground beef**
	salt and freshly ground black pepper
8	**hamburger buns**
2	**tablespoons yellow ballpark mustard**
2	**tablespoons best-quality mayonnaise**
2	**cups finely chopped iceberg lettuce**
2	**medium tomatoes, thinly sliced**
1	**large onion, thinly sliced**
1	**cup thinly sliced "hamburger" pickles**

If you're really an authentic American, you will form the 8 patties using a Tupperware hamburger patty maker. Otherwise, divide the meat into 8 equal parts. Form the meat into balls, them smash the balls between sheets of waxed paper into patties that are about 5 inches across and ½ inch thick. Season lightly with salt and generously with pepper.

Preheat a pancake griddle or large skillet. Flip the patties onto the griddle and fry until done through and brown on both sides.

Meanwhile, prepare the buns. Spread one side of each bun with mustard and the other with mayo. Layer on lettuce, tomatoes, onions, and pickles. Once the patties are cooked, transfer them to the prepared buns, slap the lids closed, and serve at once.

Per serving: 397 calories, 23 g. fat, 93 mg. cholesterol, 1,217 mg. sodium

All-American French Fries

The obvious sidedish to the All-American hamburger is french fries. The true American way is to begin with frozen french fries and serve them with plenty of salt and lots of runny catsup.

Zot's Burgers

In the green hills above Stanford University rests another institution. This college hangout, the Alpine Inn, known as Rosati's or Zot's, is known for its picnic tables under the oak trees, its beer garden atmosphere, and its trademark hamburgers.

A Zot burger is shaped like a bullet to fit inside a grilled, buttered sourdough roll. It's topped with grilled onions and served with sides of mayonnaise, tomatoes, lettuce, pickles, and raw onions, but a true Zot fan wants his burger simple. Just smoky, hot meat; limp, sweet grilled onions; and a crisp, butter-browned sourdough roll.

With such a burger under your belt, you could solve the world's problems, sitting out under the oaks in a springtime breeze.

makes 4 servings

¼	**cup dry bread crumbs**
1⅓	**pounds lean ground beef**
	salt and black pepper to taste
2	**medium onions, sliced**
4	**sourdough rolls**
2	**tablespoons butter**

Squish the bread crumbs together with the ground beef, then add salt and pepper, using lots of pepper. Shape into 4 equal-sized bullets, then place them on a hot grill.

Cook until brown and done through, turning from time to time.

While the burgers are cooking, nestle the onions up against them. Cook the onions in the drippings that come off the meat. Turn and stir the onions until they are limp and golden.

After you've turned the burgers for the last time, open the rolls, butter them, and lay them on top of the grill to brown. Then scoop the burgers into the rolls with a spatula and top with smoking hot grilled onions.

Per serving: 535 calories, 32 g. fat, 138 mg. cholesterol, 691 mg. sodium

Herb Burgers

Parsley, sage, rosemary, and thyme didn't make their first splash in the sixties. They've been combined since the middle ages by cooks and chemists making potions to ward off evil spirits and to lure love. Although we can't make any guarantees, we do believe you'll like burgers made with herbs.

And if you'd like to try a trick as old as fire, season the smoke in your barbecue grill with additional herbs. A branch of rosemary thrown on the fire will belch up a terrific aromatic black cloud that will give your burgers the most divine, pungent taste.

makes 8 servings

2½	pounds lean ground beef
¼	cup sour cream or plain nonfat yogurt
2	tablespoons fresh parsley, minced
1	teaspoon dried sage leaves, crushed
1	tablespoon fresh rosemary, minced, or ½ teaspoon dried
1	teaspoon dried thyme, crumbled salt and freshly ground pepper to taste
8	hamburger buns
¼	cup catsup

Combine beef, sour cream or yogurt, parsley, sage, rosemary, thyme, salt, and pepper. Squish the mixture together with your hands, then form into 8 1-inch-thick patties. Cover and chill at least 1 hour.

Preheat charcoal or gas grill. Place burgers on the grill, season the fire with additional herbs thrown directly onto the fire, cover, and grill the burgers, cooking about 4 minutes on each side or until cooked through. Grill the buns, cut side down, during the last 2 minutes, if desired.

Top each bun with catsup and a hot, grilled burger.

Per serving: 446 calories, 26 g. fat, 118 mg. cholesterol, 316 mg. sodium

Greek-Style Hamburgers

Use ground beef or ground lamb for this zesty Mediterranean-style hamburger. Serve the hot burgers in pita pockets along with sliced tomatoes, bell peppers, and purple onions.

makes 4 servings

Burgers:

1	**pound lean ground beef or lamb**
¼	**cup crumbled feta cheese**
½	**cup Kalamata or other black olives, finely chopped**
	salt and freshly ground black pepper to taste
4	**small pita breads, the top fourth cut off**
1	**medium tomato, thinly sliced**
1	**green or yellow bell pepper, seeded and cut into rings**
1	**small purple onion, thinly sliced**

Sauce:

8	**ounces nonfat plain yogurt**
1	**garlic clove, pressed**
2	**tablespoons fresh chopped mint**

Preheat a charcoal or gas grill. Mix together the ground meat, cheese, and olives. Season with salt and pepper. Shape into 4 thick patties.

Meanwhile, make the sauce. Stir together the yogurt, garlic, and mint. Set aside.

Grill the burgers over the hot grill about 5 inches above the coals, about 5 to 8 minutes on each side, or until cooked through, turning once.

To serve, place each cooked patty inside a pita pocket along with tomatoes, pepper rings, onions, and a generous dollop of yogurt sauce.

Per serving: 431 calories, 24 g. fat, 108 mg. cholesterol, 973 mg. sodium

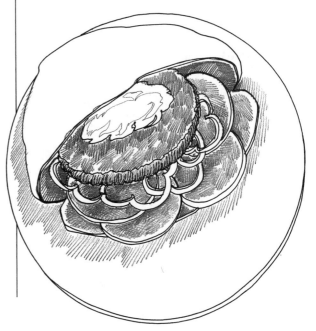

Gourmet Cheeseburgers

No kiddy burger, this is a subtle, sophisticated concoction meant for you and your best friend. Serve the burgers on sourdough rolls, covered with rich melted Gouda cheese and hidden under a ruffled lettuce petticoat with purple onion and red tomato stripes. Yumm.

makes 2 servings

½	**cup fresh sourdough bread crumbs**
2	**tablespoons minced shallots**
1	**teaspoon dried or 1 tablespoon fresh tarragon**
⅔	**pound lean ground beef**
	salt and freshly ground black pepper to taste
2	**sourdough rolls**
2	**teaspoons Dijon mustard**
2	**pieces ruffled red-tipped lettuce**
½	**medium purple onion, thinly sliced**
1	**medium tomato, thinly sliced**
1	**ounce sliced Gouda cheese**

Preheat a charcoal or gas grill. Mix the bread crumbs, shallots, tarragon, beef, salt, and pepper together. Squish it together with your hands and form into 2 1-inch-thick patties.

Grill until cooked through, about 3 to 5 minutes on each side, turning only once.

Prepare the rolls by smearing them with mustard and making a bed of lettuce, onion, and tomato.

Just before serving, top each burger with a slice of Gouda, cover the grill, and let the cheese melt, then place the cheeseburger in the bun and close. Serve at once.

Per serving: 657 calories, 31 g. fat, 136 mg. cholesterol, 1,844 mg. sodium

Fried Green Tomato Burger

Summer in the South means long twilight evenings, lightning bugs in a jar, backyard suppers where the food is laid out on red-checkered cloths, but simple dinners got up in a hurry after a long day spent putting up peaches.

Making local the idea of the hamburger, Southern mamas made hamburgers and fried green tomatoes on the stove, then served them on white bread slathered in Miracle Whip. Do not substitute mayonnaise or any of that fancy bread. Use lots of finely ground black pepper and you're in for a dinner that only calls for a tall glass of sweet iced tea with a sprig of mint stuck into the glass, a side of Mama's slang jang, and watermelon for dessert. Or maybe one of the kids will crank us some ice cream.

makes 4 servings

1½	**pounds lean ground beef**
	salt and freshly ground black pepper to taste
	vegetable oil or lard
1½	**pounds green tomatoes, thinly sliced**
½	**cup yellow cornmeal**
8	**slices white grocery-store bread**
2	**tablespoons Miracle Whip**

Shape the ground beef into 4 equal-sized patties, no more than ¾ inch thick. Season with salt and pepper. Fry them in a hot, dry skillet, just until the pinkish cast is gone in the middle, about 3 to 4 minutes on each side. Place them on a plate, cover, and keep warm.

Then, in the same skillet, heat 1 inch of oil. Dredge the tomatoes in cornmeal, salt, and pepper. Over medium-high heat, fry the tomatoes until golden. Drain them on paper towels.

To serve, slather Miracle Whip onto white bread, arrange a meat patty and a generous serving of fried green tomatoes on top, add the second piece of bread, and serve at once.

Per serving: 692 calories, 35 g. fat, 141 mg. cholesterol, 1,036 mg. sodium

Southern Fresh Relish

Mama's slang jang—an ad-lib mixture of fresh-from-the-garden peppers, cukes, tomatoes, green beans, and onions in a fresh pickle made from equal parts white vinegar and water, seasoned heavily with finely ground black pepper—could always be dredged out of the refrigerator to accompany.

California Guacamole Bacon Burger

California, home to health food and hedonism. This burger seems to me to strike a perfect balance between these two parallel world views that have always lived together comfortably in the Golden State.

makes 4 servings

Guacamole:

1	ripe Haas avocado
2	teaspoons fresh lemon juice
1	red or yellow cherry tomato, minced
¼	cup finely chopped onions
1	tablespoon minced fresh cilantro
	salt and freshly ground black pepper to taste

Burgers:

1	pound lean ground beef
4	ounces sharp white cheddar, thinly sliced
8	slices peppered bacon
2	teaspoons olive oil
4	sourdough rolls
1	cup alfalfa sprouts
1	medium tomato, thinly sliced
4	pieces butterhead lettuce

Halve, pit, and peel the avocado, then mash it with the lemon juice until nearly smooth. Stir in the tomatoes, onions, cilantro, salt, and pepper. Cover and set aside.

Shape the burgers into 4 thin, flat patties. Grill them in a hot, dry skillet just until cooked through and brown on each side. Mound cheese onto the patties, cover, and remove from the heat a few moments to let the cheese melt. At the same time, in another skillet, fry the bacon until crisp. Drain the bacon on paper towels.

To assemble, brush a little oil onto each roll, then pop in a grilled patty with cheese. Top with bacon, then layer on sprouts, tomato, and lettuce. Serve at once with a side of pickles and potato chips.

Per serving: 873 calories, 63 g. fat, 172 mg. cholesterol, 1,930 mg. sodium

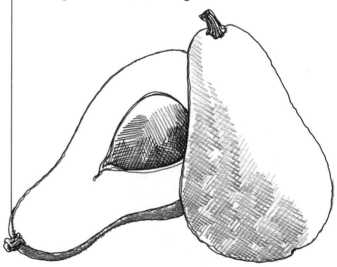

Burger Dogs

Like the shape of hot dogs? Love burgers? This one's for you.

makes 12 servings

12   pieces bacon
1½   pounds lean ground beef
¾   cup finely chopped onions
2   teaspoons German-style whole-seed mustard
      salt and freshly ground black pepper to taste
12   hot dog buns
¼   cup hot dog relish

Lay the bacon strips out on waxed paper. Crumble the ground beef in a large mixing bowl. Add ½ cup onions and the mustard. Squish it together with your hands. Season with salt and pepper. Form into 12 equal-sized balls, then roll them between the palms of your hands to form a hot dog shape.

Wrap a slice of bacon in a spiral around each burger dog, fixing both ends with toothpicks. Broil 3 inches from the heat source, rolling every minute or so, until meat is cooked and bacon is crisp.

Serve the hot burger dogs in buns slathered with relish and sprinkled with remaining ¼ cup onions.

Per serving: 605 calories, 40 g. fat, 107 mg. cholesterol, 937 mg. sodium

Barbecue Burger

Although this may sound like a redundancy, there are ways to make burgers really taste like barbecue. First off, cook them over a wood or charcoal fire scented with fruitwood smoke. Second, pump up the flavor of the meat with barbecue sauce. Last but not least, serve the burgers with plenty of thinly sliced white onions and sour pickles on toasted hamburger buns with mayonnaise and additional barbecue sauce.

makes 4 servings

Burgers:
1½   pounds lean ground beef
1   egg white, whisked until foamy
1   heel of bread, torn into small pieces
      salt and freshly ground black pepper to taste
1   tablespoon vegetable oil
½   cup minced onions
½   cup minced bell peppers
4   hamburger buns
      mayonnaise
      thin onion slices
      pickles

Barbecue Sauce:

1	**cup catsup**
½	**cup chili sauce**
¼	**cup packed brown sugar**
1	**tablespoon dry mustard**
2	**tablespoons apple-cider vinegar**
1	**tablespoon Worcestershire sauce**
	salt and freshly ground black pepper to taste
¼	**cup butter or margarine**

Crumble the ground beef. Add egg white and bread pieces and squish it all together with your hands. Season with salt and pepper, then cover and set aside.

In a small skillet over medium-high heat, sauté the onions and peppers until the onions begin to brown. Add this mixture to the meat and form into 4 1-inch-thick patties. Cover and refrigerate until the fire is prepared.

Preheat the charcoal or gas grill. While the grill is heating, make the barbecue sauce, using a pot you won't mind transferring to the grill on the barbecue. Stir together the catsup, chili sauce, brown sugar, mustard, vinegar, Worcestershire sauce, salt, and pepper. Raise to a boil over high heat at the kitchen range, add butter or margarine, then transfer to the outdoor barbecue. Let the sauce thicken there, stirring with a wooden spoon, and you'll get the greatest smoky flavor.

Grill the burgers over the preheated grill, tossing herb twigs onto the fire for aromatic smoke, about 4 minutes on each side, or until the pinkish cast is gone from the middle. Dredge the burgers in the barbecue sauce, then transfer them to hamburger buns.

Add a layer of mayonnaise plus thin slices of onion and pickle to the burgers, then serve. Pass the barbecue sauce for those who may wish to add more.

Per serving: 779 calories, 45 g. fat, 238 mg. cholesterol, 1,558 mg. sodium

Chapter Two

THE TOP TWENTY MEATLOAVES

Shaping and cooking meatloaves bring up a couple of important questions:

• Should you cook the meatloaf in a loaf pan or on a cookie sheet?

• How can you tell if it is done? Just what method gives the best results?

You'll find several different methods used in this chapter. Some recipes call for shaping the meatloaf in a loaf pan, then dumping it onto a cookie sheet for baking. This guarantees a good, crisp, brown crust over most of the meatloaf.

Other recipes call for patting the meatloaf down into a regular loaf pan. This is by far the simplest method in that you just press the mixture into the pan, pop it into the oven, and bake.

You'll be saved the risk of fat and juices dripping out onto the oven floor if you put a cookie sheet under the loaf pan. However, if you use 15 percent or leaner ground meat in the recipes, as called for, it's unlikely that you'll find too much excess fat.

If you're watching every gram of fat and cholesterol, use a bulb baster to remove the fats pooled around the edge of the meatloaf once you take it from the oven.

To make sure your meatloaf is thoroughly done in the middle—no pink—you can test it in several ways. Pierce the meatloaf and see if the juices that bubble up run clear. Or, place a meat thermometer into the thickest part and test to see that the temperature is at least 160°F. Last, you can just cut a slice out of the middle and see if it looks cooked through, in other words, the pink cast to the meat has vanished.

Remember that the denser the meatloaf, the longer it will take to cook. A standard loaf pan tightly packed may take up to 1¼ hours to bake in a 350°F oven.

If you're in a hurry, divide the meatloaf into four parts, shape into mini meatloaves, and bake on a cookie sheet with sides for about 30 minutes at 350°F. See also the microwave meatloaf recipes in this chapter for quick and easy dinners.

If you're cooking in the microwave, remember that the meat continues to cook five minutes or so after you've removed it from the microwave oven. Let the meatloaf stand before cutting or serving. It's hot!

Daddy's Texas Meatloaf

Although Daddy always made the meatloaf at our house, instead of Mama as in all those other households, he never went as far as one ardent Texas meatloaf maker who shaped the thing like the state of Texas. Oh, well, why not?

But do remember that, in Texas, we like our meatloaf made from a mixture of beef and pork, and let the cholesterol go hang.

makes 6 servings

1	**cup milk**
2	**large eggs**
¾	**cup uncooked rolled oats**
1	**pound lean ground beef**
½	**pound ground pork**
3	**tablespoons Worcestershire sauce**
1	**small tomato, diced**
½	**cup each diced celery, onions, and green bell peppers**
2	**large cloves garlic, finely chopped**
1	**tablespoon each dried basil, thyme, and oregano**
	salt and pepper to taste
4	**thick slices bacon, uncooked**
½	**cup catsup**

Preheat the oven to 425°F. In a large glass or stainless steel bowl whisk the milk and eggs together, then stir in the oats. Crumble in the ground beef and pork and mix thoroughly.

Add the Worcestershire sauce, tomatoes, celery, onions, peppers, garlic, basil, thyme, oregano, salt, and pepper. Mix well, using your hands to squish it all together.

Form into an oval loaf and place it in a 13 × 9 × 5-inch baking dish. Lay the bacon strips over the top and drizzle with the catsup. Bake until done, about 1 hour. Cool 10 minutes before serving.

Per serving: 553 calories, 37 g. fat, 215 mg. cholesterol, 967 mg. sodium

Football Friday Night Meatloaf

Here's an easy meatloaf to make for teenagers. Serve it with a mountain of mashed potatoes, peas, carrots, and plain tossed salad. It will quell the hunger of the most ravenous Friday night heroes.

makes 12 to 16 servings, enough for 1 football team plus the waterboys

½	cup honey
1	cup milk
2	large eggs
8	slices white bread
3	pounds lean ground beef
2	pounds ground pork
	salt and freshly ground black pepper to taste
2	large yellow onions, finely chopped
½	cup catsup or barbecue sauce
2	tablespoons yellow ballpark mustard

Preheat the oven to 375°F. Thoroughly grease a 12-inch round Bundt pan and set aside.

In a large glass or stainless steel bowl whisk together the honey, milk, and eggs. Tear the bread into this mixture, letting it soak up the moisture.

Crumble the beef and pork into the mixture. Season with salt and pepper. Add the onions and mix thoroughly with your hands.

Turn the mixture into the Bundt pan, pressing down firmly to pack it tight. Bake for 1¼ hours. Remove from the oven and turn the meatloaf out onto a cookie sheet with sides.

Mix the catsup or barbecue sauce and mustard together and smear it over the meatloaf. Return the meatloaf to the oven and bake an additional 15 minutes. Let it stand a few minutes before cutting.

To make it look good, fill the center hole with cooked peas and give the meatloaf a skirt of cooked carrot rings. Let it stand a few minutes before slicing.

Per serving: 596 calories, 36 g. fat, 189 mg. cholesterol, 409 mg. sodium

Meatloaf Delight

Mash potatoes to sop up this good gravy. You'll have a good dinner with no trouble at all, and almost no clean-up besides.

makes 6 servings

1	**pound lean ground beef**
1	**large yellow onion, cut into 4 thick slices**
1	**tablespoon prepared mustard**
1	**tablespoon Worcestershire sauce**
1	**dash Tabasco sauce**
1	**package onion soup mix**
1	**teaspoon capers (optional)**

Preheat the oven to 325°F. Lay out a piece of foil about 16 inches long. Form the ground beef into a loaf shape about 9 × 3 × 2 inches and lay it in the middle of the foil. Arrange slices of onion on top.

Combine mustard, Worcestershire sauce, Tabasco sauce, and soup mix and whisk together. Smear over the meatloaf. Sprinkle capers on top of the loaf, if desired. Seal up meatloaf in the foil tightly by making a drugstore wrap.

Place the foil-wrapped meatloaf on a cookie sheet and bake until done, about 1¼ hours.

Per serving: 189 calories, 12 g. fat, 61 mg. cholesterol, 153 mg. sodium

Moroccan Meatloaf

This probably is no closer to Morocco than Rick's café was, that is, no closer than the backlot in Hollywood where they made *Casablanca*. But mixing beef with lamb gives this meatloaf a decidedly exotic Middle Eastern taste.

makes 6 servings

1	**cup milk**
2	**large eggs**
½	**cup couscous**
1	**pound lean ground beef**
½	**pound ground lamb**
½	**cup each minced onions, green bell peppers, and parsley**
2	**cloves garlic, minced**
	juice and zest of half a lemon
1	**cup pine nuts**
1	**cup currants**
1	**teaspoon each ground allspice, thyme, salt, and pepper**
2	**tablespoons Worcestershire sauce**

Preheat the oven to 425°F. Whisk together in a large bowl the milk and eggs. Stir in the couscous and stir to mix. Crumble in the beef and lamb, then mix thoroughly. Add onions, peppers, and parsley. Stir in the garlic and lemon juice and zest. Mix thoroughly with your hands.

Lightly stir in the pine nuts and currants. Add allspice, thyme, salt, pepper, and Worcestershire sauce. Fold lightly. Form into an oval loaf and place on a 13 × 9 × 5-inch baking dish. Bake until done, about 1 hour. Cool 10 minutes before serving. Serve with a side dish of yogurt spiked with finely chopped cucumbers and grated carrots.

Per serving: 729 calories, 29 g. fat, 158 mg. cholesterol, 772 mg. sodium

Mediterranean Meatloaf Pinwheel

Serve this pinwheel meatloaf alongside red pepper–flecked polenta and thick slices of garden-fresh tomatoes topped with fresh basil leaves for a light summertime meatloaf.

makes 8 servings

Burgers:

1½	pounds lean ground beef
2	large eggs, lightly beaten
¾	cup tomato juice
¼	cup minced onions
4	cloves garlic, pressed
¾	cup uncooked oatmeal
	salt and freshly ground black pepper to taste

Filling:

2	tablespoons olive oil
1	rib celery and leaves, minced
½	cup finely chopped onions
¼	cup finely chopped pimiento-stuffed green olives
	salt and freshly ground black pepper to taste
1	cup dry bread crumbs
¼	cup finely chopped parsley

Preheat the oven to 350°F. Combine ground beef, eggs, tomato juice, onions, garlic, and oatmeal. Season with salt and pepper. Mix meat mixture with your hands and pat out evenly onto a 6 × 12-inch piece of waxed paper. Cover and refrigerate.

Meanwhile, in a 10-inch skillet, heat the oil, then sauté the celery, onions, and olives until the onions are translucent. Season with salt and pepper and toss with the bread crumbs and parsley.

Spread the filling evenly over the chilled meat mixture, then, using a wet spatula, roll the meatloaf up, jelly-roll fashion, starting on the long side so that you end up with a 12-inch-long loaf. Transfer the loaf to a 10 × 13-inch baking dish.

Bake until done through, about 1¼ hours. Let stand 10 minutes before slicing. Garnish with sprigs of parsley.

Per serving: 365 calories, 19 g. fat, 138 mg. cholesterol, 1,016 mg. sodium

Mideast Meatloaf

Make a pot of couscous; prepare a salad of plain yogurt, fresh mint, and cucumber; slice some red ripe tomatoes; and it's dinner from the Middle East.

makes 6 servings

4	**medium carrots, peeled**
1	**pound lean ground beef**
4	**slices day-old whole wheat bread**
1	**large egg**
1	**cup low-fat (2%) milk**
1	**tablespoon butter or margarine**
½	**cup chopped onions**
½	**cup chopped mushrooms**
2	**large mushrooms, finely sliced (optional)**
1	**tablespoon freshly grated ginger**
1	**teaspoon curry powder**
1	**teaspoon anchovy paste**
	about 1 teaspoon Dijon mustard
	sprigs of mint (optional)

Preheat the oven to 350°F. Shred carrots in a food processor fitted with the shredding disk. Add ground beef, pulse to mix, then remove to another mixing bowl.

Using the steel blade in the food processor, make crumbs from bread slices, then add egg and milk and pulse to mix. Add to carrot-beef mixture.

In a 10-inch skillet over medium heat, heat the butter or margarine and sauté the onions and mushrooms. Add ginger and curry powder and cook a minute or so longer. Stir in the anchovy paste and mustard and mix thoroughly. Add to the meat mixture and stir to mix thoroughly. Spoon the mixture into a 9 × 5-inch loaf pan and pack down using the back of a spoon. Spread the top with additional mustard. Arrange sliced mushrooms artfully over the top, if desired.

Bake until the juices run clear when pierced with a fork, about 1½ hours. Let the meatloaf stand 10 minutes before slicing. Serve each slice with a side of couscous, a sprig of mint, and a serving of cucumber dressed with plain nonfat yogurt.

Per serving: 292 calories, 16 g. fat, 111 mg. cholesterol, 230 mg. sodium

Zesty Meatloaf

Making a comeback are mother's meatloaves—slimmer, more brightly flavored, and more nutritious than ever. Serve with mashed potatoes, a green salad with carrot shards, and a cold glass of milk for Friday night's best dinner.

makes 8 servings

4	slices whole-grain bread (heels are the best)
1	can (16 ounces) tomatoes (with juice)
2	large eggs or 4 egg whites
2	pounds lean ground beef
½	green or yellow bell pepper, seeded and minced
1	jalapeño pepper, seeded and minced
2	tablespoons fresh parsley, minced
1	teaspoon dried oregano
1	teaspoon dried basil
½	teaspoon fennel seeds
2	cloves garlic, finely chopped
	salt and freshly ground black pepper to taste
3	tablespoons grated Parmesan cheese
2	tablespoons tomato sauce or catsup
½	green or yellow bell pepper, seeded and cut into rings

Preheat the oven to 350°F. Break bread into chunks in a large mixing bowl. Pour in the tomatoes and juice, breaking up the tomatoes with a spoon. Stir to soften the bread, then add the eggs and stir. Add ground beef, minced peppers, parsley, oregano, basil, and fennel seeds. Stir in the garlic, salt, and pepper, then mix thoroughly.

Press the mixture firmly into a standard loaf pan, then flip the loaf out onto a shallow baking tray with sides.

Bake until thoroughly done, about 45 minutes. Lift off any accumulated juices in the bottom of the pan. Top the loaf with Parmesan and return to the oven an additional 5 minutes or until the cheese melts.

Decorate the top of the loaf with a ribbon of tomato sauce or catsup and pepper rings. Let it stand a few minutes before serving.

Per serving: 327 calories, 21 g. fat, 165 mg. cholesterol, 334 mg. sodium

Glazed Meatloaf

This is a meatloaf like Mama made, only Mama had no microwave to speed up the process.

makes 6 servings

½   cup catsup
⅓   cup firmly packed brown sugar
¼   cup fresh lemon juice, divided
1   teaspoon Dijon mustard
1½   pounds lean ground beef
1½   cups fresh bread crumbs
¼   cup minced onions
2   egg whites, slightly beaten
1   teaspoon beef-flavored instant bouillon

Preheat the oven to 350°F. Combine the catsup, brown sugar, and 1 teaspoon lemon juice with mustard. Stir thoroughly and set aside.

Combine ground beef, remaining lemon juice, bread crumbs, onions, egg whites, and bouillon. Mix thoroughly, then add half the sauce and stir to mix thoroughly.

Place the meatloaf in a loaf pan, pressing down to make it firm. Bake 1 hour. Pour off any accumulated fat. Drizzle remaining sauce over the meat and cook 10 minutes more.

Per serving: 488 calories, 19 g. fat, 92 mg. cholesterol, 1,382 mg. sodium

To cook this dish in the microwave, mix and shape the loaf as directed, then place in a microwavable loaf pan. Microwave on 100 percent (HIGH) for 13 minutes, rotating the dish once, halfway through. Pour off any accumulated fat, then pour on the remaining sauce and microwave for an additional 3 minutes. Cover and let the meatloaf stand 5 minutes before serving.

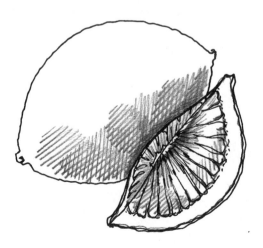

Olive Meatloaf

Serve this zesty meatloaf with mashed potatoes and a salad of red beefsteak tomatoes and fresh basil leaves drizzled with olive oil.

makes 8 servings

2	**egg whites, beaten**
½	**cup dry bread crumbs**
¼	**cup minced parsley**
½	**teaspoon dry mixed Italian herbs**
1	**cup spaghetti sauce**
2	**pounds lean ground beef**
3	**slices bacon**
1	**cup small pimiento-stuffed olives**

Preheat the oven to 350°F. Combine egg whites, bread crumbs, parsley, Italian herbs, and spaghetti sauce. Stir to mix, then add ground beef. Mix thoroughly.

Partially cook bacon in the microwave set at 100 percent (HIGH) for 1½ minutes. Drain on paper towels.

Place the meat mixture on a piece of foil and pat into a 10-inch square. Press the olives into the meat mixture, then roll the mixture, jelly-roll fashion. Place the 10 × 5-inch loaf into a loaf pan. Top with the bacon.

Bake until done through, about 1 hour. Lift the meatloaf onto a serving platter and slice into pinwheels. Garnish with additional olives.

Per serving: 428 calories, 27 g. fat, 101 mg. cholesterol, 1,046 mg. sodium

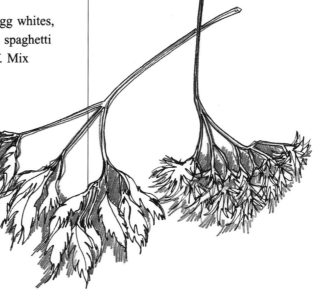

Southern Italian Meatloaf

This is what happened to Mama's meatloaf when she gave the recipe to her neighbor who'd just moved to Brooklyn from Sicily. She served this Italian-style meatloaf pinwheel with spaghetti and marinara sauce and plenty of grated Parmesan to sprinkle on top. She added hot Italian bread dripping with garlic butter and the meal was ready.

makes 6 servings

1½   pounds lean ground beef
2   eggs, lightly whisked
½   cup Italian-style bread crumbs
1   cup tomato juice
1   teaspoon salt
¼   teaspoon freshly ground black pepper
½   teaspoon dried crumbled oregano, or
     1 teaspoon fresh
½   teaspoon red pepper flakes
1   large onion, minced
2   cloves garlic, minced
1   tablespoon olive oil
4   slices thin pancetta or other boiled ham
½   cup finely chopped Italian parsley
½   cup shredded mozzarella
½   cup grated Parmesan cheese

Preheat the oven to 350°F. In a glass or stainless steel bowl crumble the meat and add the eggs, bread crumbs, tomato juice, salt, pepper, oregano, and red pepper flakes. Squish it all together with your hands. Set aside.

In a sauté pan, sauté the onions and garlic in the oil until the vegetables are translucent and beginning to brown. Add to the meatloaf and mix thoroughly.

Place a piece of plastic wrap on the counter and pat out the meatloaf into a rectangle, 9 × 14 inches. Lay out the pancetta strips on the meatloaf. Sprinkle the parsley onto the ham. Then sprinkle the top with the two cheeses, reserving a little.

Lift the plastic wrap to help you roll the meatloaf, jelly-roll style, then roll it off the plastic wrap and into a 9 × 5 × 3-inch loaf pan. Sprinkle remaining cheeses on the top and bake until done, about 1¼ hours. Let it stand a few minutes before serving.

Per serving: 550 calories, 35 g. fat, 225 mg. cholesterol, 1,525 mg. sodium

Creole Meatloaves

Shape these into four miniloaves. Brown and cook with a Creole-style sauce for the main course in a menu that begs for perfect rice and a side dish of okra.

makes 4 servings

1	**pound lean ground beef**
2	**heels of bread, torn into pieces**
2	**egg whites, whisked until foamy**
	salt and freshly ground black pepper to taste

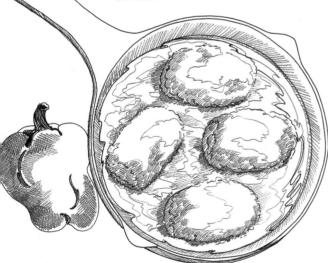

½	**cup chopped onions**
1	**tablespoon cornstarch**
1	**can (15 ounces) stewed tomatoes (with juice)**
1	**can (14½ ounces) beef stock**
1	**teaspoon dried oregano**
1	**teaspoon sugar**
½	**teaspoon hot-pepper sauce (or to taste)**
1	**large green bell pepper, seeded and diced**

Crumble the ground beef. Add bread and egg whites and mix well. Season with salt and pepper. Shape into 4 miniloaves.

In a large skillet, heated over medium-high heat, brown the loaves. Remove them from the skillet and set aside.

Cook the onions in the pan drippings, adding a little oil, if necessary, to keep them from sticking. Stir in the cornstarch, then add the tomatoes and juice, stock, oregano, sugar, and hot-pepper sauce. Stir and cook until the mixture boils. Slip the meatloaves into the sauce, reduce heat, cover, and simmer for 15 minutes. Add the peppers, cook an additional 3 minutes, and remove from the heat.

Serve each meatloaf with sauce over cooked rice.

Per serving: 376 calories, 19 g. fat, 92 mg. cholesterol, 438 mg. sodium

Salisbury Meatloaves

Cook up a batch of mashed potatoes. Add some green beans and you have a diner-style meal right at home.

makes 6 servings

1	can (10¾ ounces) onion soup
1½	pounds lean ground beef
2	heels of bread, torn into pieces
1	egg
	salt and freshly ground black pepper to taste
3	large onions, thinly sliced
1	tablespoon flour
½	teaspoon Dijon mustard
¼	cup catsup
1	teaspoon Worcestershire sauce

Combine ¼ cup of the soup with ground beef, bread pieces, egg, salt, and pepper. Squish it together with your hands, then shape into 6 miniloaves. In a large skillet heated over medium-high heat, brown the loaves then remove them from the skillet.

Place the onions in the skillet, turn the heat down to medium, cover, and cook the onions until they are wilted and beginning to brown, at least 10 minutes, stirring from time to time.

Add the flour to the remaining soup in the can and stir to make a smooth sauce. Stir in the mustard, catsup, and Worcestershire sauce. Pour this mixture over the cooking onions, stir, and bring to a boil. Reduce the heat, place the meatloaves in the pan, cover, and simmer for 15 minutes, stirring the gravy occasionally. Serve with a side of mashed potatoes.

Per serving: 354 calories, 22 g. fat, 138 mg. cholesterol, 825 mg. sodium

Up-Against-the-Wall Meatloaves

Here's an emergency dinner you can make when there's hardly anything in the refrigerator-freezer but a pound of ground beef and some frozen vegetables. Remember, you can easily thaw ground beef in the microwave.

One pound of ground beef will thaw in 10 minutes. For the first 5 minutes, set the microwave at 30 percent (MED-LOW); for the next 5 minutes, set it at 10 percent (LOW). Mix the meatloaf and microwave it, and you've made a quick and easy dinner with very little cleanup for your trouble.

makes 4 servings

1	**pound ground beef**
¾	**cup frozen peas**
¾	**cup frozen carrots**
1	**small onion, diced**
2	**heels of bread, torn to pieces**
2	**eggs**
	salt and pepper to taste
2	**tablespoons catsup**

Crumble the ground beef, then add the peas, carrots, onions, bread pieces, and eggs. Mix lightly with a fork, then add salt and pepper. Shape the mixture into 4 miniloaves. Place the loaves on a microwavable dish, then cook, covered, 10 minutes on 100 percent (HIGH). Let the loaves rest 5 minutes before serving. While they're resting, squiggle a line of catsup down the center of each one.

Per serving: 388 calories, 22 g. fat, 229 mg. cholesterol, 528 mg. sodium

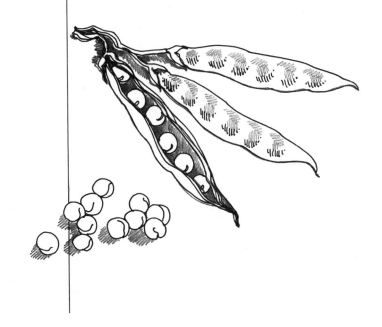

Meatloaf Strata

Most supermarkets sell a ground meat product they call meatloaf mix. Generally, it's some mixture of ground beef, pork, and/or veal. If your market sells this, you're halfway home to a terrific meatloaf. If you can't buy this product, combine 1 pound ground beef with ½ pound each ground veal and pork to make your own meatloaf mix.

This meatloaf tastes great the second day, and it freezes well, so go ahead and make the whole thing, even if you have a small family. You'll get a free lunch out of it.

You could slice it cold and make sandwiches for packed lunches that would play well at work and in the school cafeteria.

makes 8 servings

2	**pounds mixed ground meats**
2	**cups soft rye bread crumbs**
1	**egg white, whisked until foamy**
1	**can (5.33 ounces) evaporated milk**
¾	**cup fresh chopped parsley**
2	**tablespoons olive oil**
½	**pound fresh mushrooms, thinly sliced**
1	**small onion, thinly sliced**
½	**teaspoon dried summer savory**
½	**teaspoon dillweed**
½	**cup grated Romano cheese**

Preheat the oven to 350°F. Crumble the ground meat. Stir in the bread crumbs, egg white, and milk. Stir in half the parsley, cover, and refrigerate.

In a large skillet, heat the oil over medium-high heat, then sauté the mushrooms, onions, savory, and dill until the onions are beginning to brown. Remove from the heat. Toss in the remaining parsley and the Romano cheese and stir.

Pack half the meat mixture into a 9 × 5 × 3-inch loaf pan. Make an even layer of the mushroom mixture, then cover with the remaining meat mixture.

Bake until done, about 1¼ hours. Pour off excess fat and let the meatloaf stand a few minutes before slicing.

Per serving: 589 calories, 31 g. fat, 161 mg. cholesterol, 1,347 mg. sodium

Meatloaf Pot Roast

A midwinter dinner made in a cast iron Dutch oven, all this meatloaf calls for to accompany it is a big pan of cornbread and a cold glass of milk. Children love this mixture of meat and vegetables cooked together so that the good meat drippings flavor the vegetables.

makes 6 servings

1½   pounds lean ground beef
2   heels of bread, torn into small pieces
½   cup low-fat (2%) milk
1   egg white, whisked until frothy
      salt and freshly ground black pepper to taste
¼   cup minced onions
1   teaspoon Worcestershire sauce
½   teaspoon Dijon mustard
4   cups peeled raw vegetables, cut into uniform
      large chunks: potatoes, rutabagas, carrots,
      onions, turnips, celery
1   can (14½ ounces) beef stock
2   tablespoons flour
½   cup water

Crumble the ground beef. Add bread pieces, milk, and egg white. Season with salt and pepper, then add onions, Worcestershire sauce, and mustard. Squish it together with your hands.

Form the meat into a loaf shape and refrigerate a few minutes. Then preheat a dry Dutch oven and brown the meatloaf on all sides over medium-high heat. Lift it out of the pan. Make a bed of the vegetables. Place the meatloaf back onto the vegetables, pour the stock over them, cover, and turn the heat down to a simmer. Cook until the meatloaf is done, about 1 hour.

To serve, lift the meat and vegetables onto a platter and keep warm. Make a gravy from the good pan drippings by dissolving 2 tablespoons flour into ½ cup water, then pour it into the drippings. Raise to a boil, stirring, taste, and adjust the seasonings. Serve this gravy alongside the platter of meat and vegetables.

Per serving: 349 calories, 20 g. fat, 140 mg. cholesterol, 306 mg. sodium

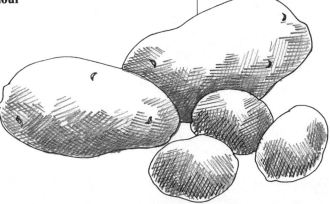

Manhattan Meatloaf

The list of ingredients here is so long, it looks more like a shopping list than a recipe, but it's worth every last item. Serve this uptown meatloaf with boiled new potatoes and steamed green beans, and you can offer it to company.

makes 8 servings

Seasoning Mix:

1	tablespoon dry mustard
2	teaspoons paprika
1	teaspoon salt
1	teaspoon dried thyme leaves
2	teaspoons sweet basil
1	teaspoon pepper
½	teaspoon white pepper

Meatloaf:

8	thick slices of peppered bacon
2	medium onions, coarsely chopped
1	medium bell pepper, seeded and coarsely chopped
2	ribs celery and leaves, coarsely chopped
4	bay leaves
2	cloves garlic, chopped
1	cup tomato juice
1	can (5.33 ounces) evaporated milk
1½	pounds lean ground beef
½	pound ground veal
2	eggs, lightly beaten
12	saltine crackers, mashed into crumbs

Preheat the oven to 350°F. Combine the seasoning mix, stirring together the mustard, paprika, salt, thyme, basil, and peppers. Set aside.

In a large skillet over medium-high heat, cook the bacon until crisp and brown, taking care not to burn it. Lift the bacon with a slotted spoon into a large mixing bowl, break into bite-sized pieces, and reserve.

Add the onions to the bacon grease and cook until they're golden brown. Add the peppers, celery, bay leaves, garlic, and 2 tablespoons of the seasoning mix and cook about 4 minutes, stirring as it cooks. Add remaining seasoning mix and continue cooking about 5 minutes. Remove from the heat. Fish out the bay leaves and discard them.

Pour tomato juice and milk over the cooked bacon. Add the cooked vegetables and blend well. Crumble in the ground meats and stir. Add eggs and cracker crumbs and mix thoroughly.

Form into a loaf shape and pack into a 3-quart casserole dish. Bake until done, about 1 hour. Let the meatloaf stand about 10 minutes before slicing.

Per serving: 687 calories, 42 g. fat, 199 mg. cholesterol, 1,368 mg. sodium

Bettie Henry's Dinner Party Meatloaf

Bettie sometimes cooks this in the microwave at 100 percent (HIGH) power for 20 minutes, turning every 4 minutes. She does this when she has such a busy dinner party cooking schedule that the oven is full of other good things to eat.

Baked or microwaved, this meatloaf is definitely good enough for guests. And easy, too.

makes 8 servings

1	pound lean ground beef
1	pound ground turkey
1	pound ground turkey sausage
4	slices whole wheat bread, cubed
4	egg whites, whisked until foamy
1	teaspoon pepper
2	tablespoons catsup
2	teaspoons low-sodium soy sauce
2	teaspoons Worcestershire sauce
2	teaspoons lemon juice
2	teaspoons parsley, finely chopped
12	shallots, coarsely chopped

Preheat the oven to 350°F. Crumble the ground meats. Sprinkle bread pieces over the meat and stir in the egg whites. Add pepper, catsup, soy sauce, Worcestershire sauce, lemon juice, parsley, and shallots. Mix thoroughly.

Pack this meatloaf into a 9 × 5 × 3-inch loaf pan, then turn it upside down onto a baking sheet with sides. Bake until done, about 1¼ hours. Let the meatloaf stand 10 minutes or so before slicing. It's good hot or cold.

Per serving: 543 calories, 39 g. fat, 112 mg. cholesterol, 653 mg. sodium

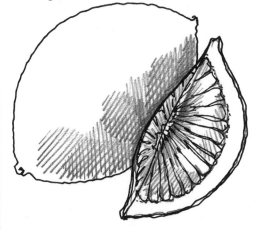

Hamburger Croquettes

Here's a new lower-fat rendition of an old family favorite that you can make ahead, then finish in less than 20 minutes once you're ready to serve.

makes 4 servings

1	pound lean ground beef
2	tablespoons low-fat or fat-free mayonnaise
½	cup bread crumbs
¼	cup diced green onions and tops
4	tablespoons minced parsley
	salt and freshly ground black pepper to taste
	few dashes of red-pepper sauce
1	egg white
1	teaspoon each dried basil and oregano
1	can (16 ounces) tomatoes (with juice)
	lemon peel twists and parsley sprigs

Heat a 10-inch skillet over medium heat, then cook ground beef just until it loses its pink cast.

Meanwhile, mix the mayonnaise and half the bread crumbs, onions, and parsley. Then add black pepper, salt, and red-pepper sauce. Stir in the egg white.

Drain the ground beef, then add to the mayonnaise mixture. Stir thoroughly, then shape into 4 patties. Coat with the remaining bread crumbs. Cover and refrigerate at least 30 minutes.

In a small saucepan combine basil, oregano, and tomatoes and juice, breaking up the tomatoes with a spoon, then add the remaining onions and parsley. Simmer 10 minutes, taste, and adjust seasonings with salt and pepper.

Twenty minutes before serving time, remove the patties from the refrigerator and broil them 6 inches from heat source until lightly browned, about 5 minutes on each side.

To serve, pool warm sauce on a dinner plate then place a steaming brown pattie on top and garnish with a twist of lemon peel and a sprig of parsley.

Per serving: 420 calories, 26 g. fat, 160 mg. cholesterol, 887 mg. sodium

Mini Microwave Meat-and-Cheese Loaves

Serve with spinach and mashed potatoes and a side of cold pickled beets for a Scandinavian-style dinner.

makes 2 servings

½	**pound lean ground beef**
4	**ounces nökkelost or Swiss cheese, shredded**
2	**tablespoons chopped green onions and tops**
1	**tablespoon milk**
1	**tablespoon crushed rye crackers**
	salt and pepper to taste

Stir ground beef and half the cheese together with onions, milk, crackers, salt, and pepper. Divide the meat mixture in half and form into small loaves.

Place the loaves on a microwavable dish. Cover with waxed paper and microwave at 100 percent (HIGH) for 2 minutes. Rotate the dish half a turn and cook 2 minutes more. Sprinkle the remaining cheese on top of the loaves and let them stand 5 minutes before serving.

Per serving: 494 calories, 34 g. fat, 143 mg. cholesterol, 825 mg. sodium

Kid's Meatloaf

Sometimes, kids are intimidated by adult-sized servings. Why not make your baby queen her own mini-meatloaf, folding in all the good nutrition she ought to have into one irresistible dish, just for her. If you want to add a couple of tablespoons of peas to her dinner, just nestle them around the meatloaf before cooking and cook everything at once.

makes 1 toddler-sized serving

¼	**cup lean ground beef**
1	**egg white**
½	**cup assorted grated vegetables: carrots, onions, celery**
2	**saltine crackers, crumbled**
1	**tablespoon catsup**

Stir ground beef and egg white together with grated vegetables and crackers. Form into a miniloaf and place in a microwavable dish.

Squiggle a line of catsup down the middle of the meatloaf, cover, and microwave at 100 percent (HIGH) for 3 minutes. Let it stand 5 minutes before serving.

Per serving: 423 calories, 16 g. fat, 46 mg. cholesterol, 669 mg. sodium

Chapter Three

THE TOP TWENTY CASSEROLES AND STIR-FRIES

Perhaps in casseroles and stir-fries we have the best examples of classic recipes made new simply by the exchange of lower-fat beef for old-fashioned fatty hamburger.

Make the Tamale Pie in this book and you'll see that the new slimmed-down version is long on grain and short on fats, but really intense when it comes to flavors. It's one of our family's favorites, and we recommend it without reservation.

We also like Roberta Wallace's Upside-Down Hamburger Pie (see page 72), which puts the ground beef on the bottom and the rice in the middle. It makes a lovely dish to take to a potluck or picnic. Tasty either hot or at room temperature, it's a dish that's sure to please a family.

Many of the recipes in this section have been updated, calling for more vegetables and grains and less meat so that you get a more complete, more balanced dinner for your time and trouble.

Tamale Pie

Tamale Pie is almost as American as apple pie. At least to those of us who grew up in the Southwest, this suppertime standby was as common as Kraft dinners and equally welcome.

Substitute freely between bell pepper and celery, using what you have on hand to make ½ cup total. Use canned refritos (refried beans) if you must, but you'll save the most money and get the best taste if you use cooked and refried dried pinto beans. The salsa can be fresh or canned. For cheese, use cheddar or a mix of cheeses you have on hand. Although we prefer homemade cornbread batter—cheaper and tastier—you can plug in a 15-ounce box of cornbread mix. It will have too much sugar, and that would make any Tex-Mex cowboy scream *caramba,* but it is fast.

makes 8 servings

1	**cup dried pinto beans (or 1 15-ounce can refried beans)**
1	**pound lean ground beef**
½	**cup chopped onions**
½	**cup chopped bell peppers and/or celery**
½	**cup chunky salsa (mild or hot)**
½	**cup (2.25-ounce can) sliced ripe olives salt and pepper to taste cornbread batter (see following recipe) or a 15-ounce mix**
¾	**cup grated cheddar or a mixture of cheese**

Make refritos by first cooking a cup of dried pintos in boiling, salted water to cover until tender, about 2 hours. Then drain and mash the beans in an oiled skillet over medium heat, until cooked and dry.

Preheat the oven to 350°F. Sauté beef with onions and peppers and/or celery in a 10-inch skillet over medium-high heat, stirring, until meat is cooked through and vegetables are translucent. Drain off any fat. Stir in salsa and olives. Season with salt and pepper.

Spray a 9-inch deep-dish pie pan with vegetable nonstick spray. Cover the bottom and sides of the pan with refried beans. Then pour meat mixture over that. Top with cornbread batter. Sprinkle with cheese, then bake until crust is lightly browned, about 30 to 35 minutes.

Allow the pie to rest 10 minutes on a rack before cutting into pie slices. Serve, garnished with shredded iceberg lettuce and chopped tomatoes, if desired.

Per serving: 463 calories, 23 g. fat, 104 mg. cholesterol, 1,164 mg. sodium

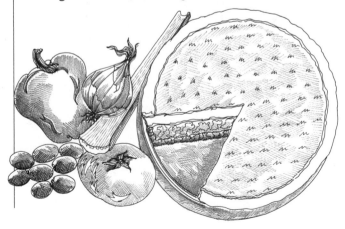

Cornbread Topping

This cornbread is terrific made all by itself in a black skillet, too.

makes 8 servings

3   **tablespoons bacon grease or vegetable oil**
1   **cup yellow cornmeal**
½   **cup unbleached white flour**
½   **teaspoon each salt, baking soda, and baking powder**
1   **tablespoon sugar**
1   **cup buttermilk**
1   **egg**

Heat bacon grease or oil until smoking hot. Meanwhile, combine cornmeal, flour, salt, baking soda, baking powder, and sugar and stir to mix. Stir in buttermilk and egg and mix thoroughly. Pour in hot bacon grease and stir.

Layer this cornbread batter over the meat mixture in Tamale Pie (see recipe above) and bake.

Dress this cornbread topping up by crumbling a piece of bacon into the batter or adding a couple tablespoons chopped onions and/or bell peppers or a tablespoon of chili powder. If you like your food picante, chip in a fresh jalapeño. If you wish to bake this as plain, country cornbread, preheat the oven to 400°F, heat the bacon grease in a black cast-iron skillet, and bake the bread in the hot skillet. It takes only about 10 to 12 minutes. The top will be dull. Run it under the broiler to brown, then serve immediately with plenty of sweet butter and syrup for supper.

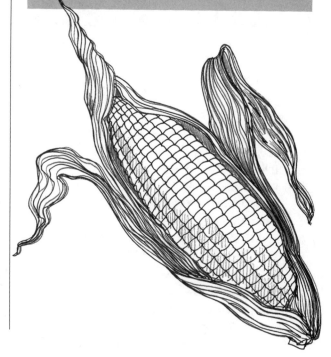

Homemade Hamburger's Assistant

Believe me, you can help hamburger without letting some manufacturer do your thinking for you. Make your own hamburger's assistant. Then brown the meat with an onion. Cook a pot of noodles, rice, or spaghetti—depending on what you have in the larder—and you've not only helped the hamburger, you've helped the grocery budget and the family's health.

This home-made hamburger helper wouldn't be any bargain if you looked over the long list of spices and herbs, then took off for the local supermarket to buy those products in lovely little glass jars. The way to beat that system is to shop your local food co-op where the herbs and spices are sold in bulk.

When I looked over the list, I only had about half the herbs. But a trip to the local food co-op and purchase of a couple of scoops of each herb resulted in a bill of less than $2, and I had plenty of each herb left over to restock my basic pantry. Store the herbs in baby food jars, well labeled, and you've saved yourself a bundle.

makes 1½ ounces, enough to season 7 pounds of meat

1	tablespoon dried basil leaves, crumbled
2	tablespoons dried oregano
¼	cup dried parsley
1	teaspoon fennel seeds
1	teaspoon savory
1	teaspoon marjoram
½	teaspoon red-pepper flakes
1	tablespoon coarsely ground black pepper
1	tablespoon salt
1	teaspoon sugar
1	teaspoon garlic salt

Combine these spices in a clean, airtight jar and store in the pantry.

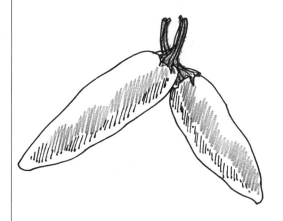

Good and Cheap Hamburger Stir-Fry

serves 4

1   pound lean ground beef
1   medium onion, chopped
1   tablespoon (or to taste) Homemade Hamburger's Assistant spice mix
1   can (16 ounces) tomatoes (with juice)
12   ounces spaghetti or noodles
     grated Parmesan cheese

In a 10-inch skillet or wok over medium-high heat, brown the hamburger along with onions and spice mix. Add tomatoes and juice, breaking up the tomatoes with a spoon, then turn heat to low and simmer about 10 minutes, adjusting seasonings to taste.

Meanwhile, in a large pot of boiling, slightly salted water cook noodles or spaghetti just until barely cooked. Drain.

To serve, arrange pasta on a large serving platter and top with sauce. Dust the top with Parmesan.

Per serving: 388 calories, 20 g. fat, 95 mg. cholesterol, 298 mg. sodium

Beefy Potato Empanadas

Empanadas are Latin America's hot dog, sold at train stations, at soccer games, and on street corners. Use a food processor to mash the potatoes and make the pastry. Serve piping hot with a side of salsa.

makes 10 6-inch pies

Filling:
2   medium potatoes, peeled
½   teaspoon salt
1   teaspoon red-pepper flakes
3   tablespoons vegetable oil
1   large yellow onion, finely chopped
½   medium green bell pepper, seeded and finely chopped
1   jalapeño pepper, seeded and finely chopped
½   teaspoon ground cumin
½   teaspoon cayenne pepper
¾   pound ground beef
1   cup fresh, frozen, or canned corn kernels
1   cup grated Monterey Jack or Mexican white cheese
     salt and freshly ground black pepper to taste

Pastry:
1   cup warm water
1   teaspoon white vinegar
1   teaspoon salt
3½ cups unbleached white flour
     vegetable oil

To make the filling, cover potatoes with water and cook until tender in a medium saucepan with salt and red-pepper flakes.

Meanwhile, in a 10-inch skillet, heat oil over medium-high heat, sauté onions and peppers with cumin and cayenne until vegetables are limp and beginning to brown. Add ground beef and cook until no longer pink. Add corn and continue cooking for 5 minutes. Remove from heat and stir in cheese.

Remove potatoes to the food processor and puree using the steel blade, then combine with other vegetables and meat. Add just enough of the potato cooking water to make a thick paste. Adjust seasonings with salt and pepper.

Make pastry in the food processor fitted with the steel blade after you've wiped out the bowl. Combine water, vinegar, salt, flour, and 3 tablespoons oil, then process to make a ball that rides the blade around and cleans the sides of the bowl, about 20 seconds.

Divide the dough into 10 equal pieces and roll each into a 6-inch circle on a lightly floured surface. Place ½ cup filling on each circle, leaving a ½-inch border. Wet the border to help seal the dough, then fold over to form semicircles and crimp the edges with the tines of a fork.

In about an inch of oil heated to 360°F fry both sides of the pastry until golden, about 5 minutes, then drain on paper towels. Serve with fresh salsa.

Per serving: 400 calories, 21 g. fat, 49 mg. cholesterol, 679 mg. sodium

Not So Original Joe's

Bettie Henry, who gave me her version of a classic northern California dish, has made some improvements old Joe never thought of. She's doubled the amount of spinach in the dish. She's dusted the finished product with Parmesan cheese. She's added a squeeze of lemon juice. Believe me, this is a one-dish dinner that has everything. Good taste, good nutrition, good enough for those who are really short of time and patience—a noncook's dream. Serve with thick slices of crusty French bread.

Bettie Henry's Take On Original Joe's Special

makes 6 servings

¾   **pound lean ground beef**
2   **large yellow onions, cut into thick slices**
3   **cloves garlic, minced**
½   **teaspoon fresh oregano leaves**
2   **bunches of spinach, carefully washed and dried, or 2 packages frozen**
3   **large eggs, slightly beaten**
     juice and zest of half a lemon
     salt and freshly ground black pepper to taste
     Parmesan cheese

Sauté the meat over medium heat in a 12-inch skillet or wok. Once meat begins to lose its pink color, add the onions and garlic and continue to cook until the onions have turned translucent and are beginning to brown.

Meanwhile, in a large stew pot of barely salted water that is at a rolling boil, drop in spinach leaves and cook 3 minutes, then lift the leaves out and refresh under cold water. Drain. Chop the spinach coarsely. (If you're using frozen spinach, skip this step and start by squeezing liquid out of the chopped spinach.)

Turn the heat under the skillet to the lowest setting, then add spinach, eggs, lemon juice and zest, salt, and pepper. Cook and toss just until the eggs are cooked.

Remove the mixture to a warmed platter, dust the top generously with Parmesan, and serve at once.

Per serving: 215 calories, 15 g. fat, 191 mg. cholesterol, 403 mg. sodium

Cazuela Sabrosa

Here's an easy casserole to feed the family or to take to a potluck. You don't even have to parboil the pasta. Just add uncooked macaroni or rigatoni to the dish and it will cook in the wonderful juices of the casserole. You can control the "heat" in the dish by choosing to add or not add the jalapeño. All you need to complete this meal is a green salad with a simple vinaigrette dressing.

makes 10 servings

1   medium onion, thinly sliced
4   cloves garlic, minced
2   ribs celery, cut into bite-sized pieces
1   medium green bell pepper, seeded and chopped
1   fresh jalapeño pepper, seeded and chopped (optional)
1   tablespoon olive oil
1   pound lean ground beef
2   cups fresh, frozen, or canned corn, drained
2   cups chopped tomatoes or 1 can (16 ounces) with juice
1   can (4½ ounces) diced green chilies
1   cup black olives, drained
1   cup uncooked rigatoni or macaroni
1   tablespoon chili powder
        salt and pepper to taste
1   cup plain nonfat yogurt or buttermilk
2   cups grated Monterey Jack cheese
        fresh cilantro leaves

Preheat the oven to 350°F. Sauté onions, garlic, celery, bell peppers, and jalapeños in oil in a large skillet over medium-high heat, until the onions are beginning to brown.

Add beef and brown it evenly, breaking it up as necessary. Then stir in corn, tomatoes, green chilies, olives, pasta, chili powder, salt, pepper, and yogurt or buttermilk.

Pour into a 13 × 9 × 2½-inch baking dish. Top with cheese and bake, covered, until the pasta is done and the liquid is absorbed, about 45 minutes. Remove the cover and let it stand a few minutes before serving. Garnish each serving with cilantro leaves. Serve at once.

Per serving: 398 calories, 25 g. fat, 82 mg. cholesterol, 726 mg. sodium

Hamburger Pâté

Here's where that food processor comes in handy. By processing chicken livers to combine with well-seasoned ground beef, you can create a luscious country pâté that makes a great cold sandwich on dark brown bread, slathered with Dijon mustard, and served with butterhead lettuce and cornichons on the side.

makes 12 servings

¼	pound chicken livers, fat removed, rinsed and dried
¾	cup low-fat (2%) milk
1	large egg
4	slices day-old French bread
4	medium carrots, peeled
½	cup finely chopped fresh parsley
1	teaspoon salt
¼	teaspoon freshly ground black pepper
¼	teaspoon ground allspice
1	medium onion
1	cup fresh mushrooms
2	cloves garlic
1	tablespoon butter or margarine
¼	cup brandy (optional)
1	pound lean ground beef
½	cup shelled pistachio nuts
1	tablespoon Dijon mustard

Preheat the oven to 350°F. Fit the food processor bowl with the steel blade and pulse the chicken livers to a coarse puree. Add milk and egg and pulse to mix. Remove to a large mixing bowl.

Using the processor, make bread crumbs. Remove them to the mixing bowl. Using the grating disk, grate the carrots and add them to the mixing bowl. Stir in parsley, salt, pepper, and allspice. Stir and set aside.

Chop the onion, mushrooms, and garlic in the food processor using the steel blade. Heat a 10-inch skillet with the butter or margarine over medium-high heat, then sauté the onions, mushrooms, and garlic until golden brown, about 5 minutes. Add brandy, if desired, and cook 30 seconds. Pour into the livers and milk mixture. Stir well, then add ground beef and half the pistachios, mixing thoroughly.

Spoon the mixture into a 9 × 5-inch loaf pan, pressing it down with the back of the spoon. Spread the top with mustard. Add the remaining pistachio nuts, arranging them artfully on the top. Bake until the juices run clear, about 1½ hours. Cool on a rack, then cover and refrigerate until serving time. Cut into thin slices to serve.

Per serving: 238 calories, 13 g. fat, 88 mg. cholesterol, 398 mg. sodium

Reneé Andrews Burrito Bake

Ever notice how you seem to have 2 flour tortillas left over in the pack that seem to be going to waste? Here's Reneé Andrews' quick and easy one-dish supper that makes great use of those leftover tortillas.

makes 4 servings

½	**pound lean ground beef**
1	**medium onion, finely chopped**
1	**garlic clove, finely chopped**
¼	**teaspoon cayenne pepper**
½	**teaspoon seasoned salt**
¼	**cup water**
1	**can (16 ounces) refried beans**
2	**large flour tortillas**
1¼	**cups shredded cheddar cheese**

Preheat the oven to 350°F. In a 10-inch skillet over medium-high heat, brown the meat. Drain any fat that remains in the skillet. Add onions, garlic, cayenne, and seasoned salt to the ground beef. Cook and stir 3 minutes, then add water. Bring to a boil, then reduce heat and simmer, uncovered, for 10 minutes.

Meanwhile, heat refried beans in the microwave for 2 minutes at 100 percent (HIGH), or in a pan over medium heat for 10 minutes.

Lightly grease a 2-quart round casserole dish. Heat 1 tortilla in the microwave at 100 percent (HIGH) for 15 seconds, or in a dry skillet over high heat for about a minute, then place the tortilla in the bottom of the casserole. Spread the beans over the tortilla, spoon the ground beef mixture over the beans, then layer 1 cup cheese over the beef.

Heat the second tortilla as before, then place over the cheese. Top with remaining cheese.

Bake until bubbly and the cheese is beginning to brown, 10 to 15 minutes.

Per serving: 611 calories, 33 g. fat, 121 mg. cholesterol, 1,197 mg. sodium

You can make this dish ahead of time. Instead of baking, cover it and keep it in the refrigerator for a day.

If you wish to make the dish look spectacular when serving, shave some iceberg lettuce, chop some tomatoes, and dredge up some black olives and a spot of sour cream. Arrange the lettuce on the dinner plate, add a wedge of the casserole, then top with fresh tomatoes, a black olive, and a dollop of sour cream.

Red Flannel Hamburger Hash

Easy to prepare and as comfortable as your favorite pair of slippers, this is a good way to make use of leftover cooked red potatoes. You can, of course, substitute white, yellow, or russets, if that's what you have on hand.

makes 4 servings

1	**pound lean ground beef**
1	**large onion, finely chopped**
4	**cloves garlic, finely chopped**
1	**rib celery with leaves, finely chopped**
2	**cups cubed cooked red potatoes**
¼	**cup minced parsley**
⅔	**cup chicken broth**
	salt and freshly ground black pepper to taste
1½	**tablespoons bread crumbs**
	catsup

In a 10-inch cast-iron skillet over medium heat, sauté the ground beef along with the onions, garlic, and celery. Once onions begin to brown, stir in the potatoes, parsley, and broth. Season with salt and pepper and remove from the heat.

Preheat the oven to 350°F. Smooth the top of the meat mixture in the skillet, sprinkle with bread crumbs, then bake for 20 minutes. Decorate the top with catsup and serve.

Per serving: 380 calories, 20 g. fat, 93 mg. cholesterol, 533 mg. sodium

Bettie's Chilaquiles

Long used in Mexico to make one more meal from stale tortillas, this easy-to-make casserole simmers wedges of tortilla in a chile-flavored broth until the mixture takes on the texture of a casserole. Bettie jazzes up her version by sprinkling the top with cheese and running it under the broiler until it bubbles.

Because this dish freezes so well, I've given you a recipe that will serve 8 to 10. Freeze what you don't eat tonight in a microwavable casserole dish, covered tightly with microwave plastic wrap, and you have one free lunch just waiting to be baked. To complete this dinner, tear some lettuce leaves for a salad, make iced tea, and it's done.

makes 8 to 10 servings

¾	**pound lean ground beef**
1	**medium onion, chopped**
2	**garlic cloves, pressed**
2	**tablespoons (or to taste) chili powder**
	salt and pepper to taste
1	**cup hot water**
6	**day-old corn tortillas**
1	**can (16 ounces) Mexican-style tomatoes (with juice)**
1	**can (2¼ ounces) sliced black olives**
1	**cup grated cheddar cheese**

In a hot 10-inch, ovenproof skillet, brown the meat along with the onions, garlic, and chili powder. Season with salt and pepper, then pour in water and boil for 5 minutes.

Meanwhile, stack the tortillas and cut the stack into wedges. Each tortilla should yield 6 wedges, giving you 36 wedges all together. Add the tortilla wedges along with the tomatoes and juice to the skillet, and boil, covered, until the liquid is nearly absorbed, about 10 minutes.

Sprinkle the top with olives and cheddar. Run the skillet under the broiler until the top is bubbly and brown. Serve in soup bowls. A sprig of cilantro makes a nice garnish.

Per serving: 203 calories, 8 g. fat, 31 mg. cholesterol, 260 mg. sodium

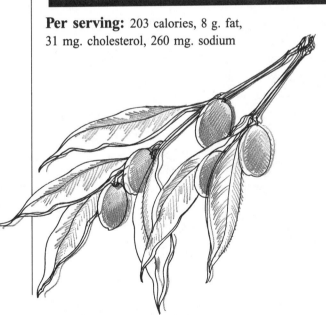

Spring Pasta With Green and Red Meat Sauce

Colorful zucchini coins nestled in a red meat sauce make this a bright, rich sauce for spaghetti.

makes 6 servings

2	tablespoons olive oil
1	large leek with 1-inch green stem, thinly sliced
4	cloves garlic, minced
1	medium zucchini, sliced into ¼-inch-thick coins
¾	pound lean ground beef
1	cup chopped fresh parsley
1	teaspoon dried basil, crumbled
1	teaspoon dried oregano, crumbled
1	teaspoon paprika
½	teaspoon sugar
	salt and pepper to taste
1	can (28 ounces) Italian plum tomatoes (with juice), chopped
1	can (6 ounces) tomato paste
¾	cup dry red wine or beef broth
	juice of half a lemon
1	pound fusille or other pasta, cooked al dente
½	cup freshly grated Parmesan cheese

Heat oil in a 12-inch skillet over medium-high heat. Add leeks, garlic, and zucchini and sauté until the leeks are tender and beginning to brown. Stir in beef, half the parsley, then add basil, oregano, and paprika and continue cooking 1 minute.

Stir in sugar, salt, pepper, tomatoes and juice, tomato paste, wine or broth, and lemon juice. Stir thoroughly. Reduce heat and simmer, uncovered, while the pasta cooks and until the sauce is thick, about 20 minutes. Taste and correct seasonings.

To serve, drain pasta, then toss with half the Parmesan, then half the remaining parsley and the sauce. Top with remaining Parmesan and parsley and serve.

Per serving: 396 calories, 19 g. fat, 62 mg. cholesterol, 538 mg. sodium

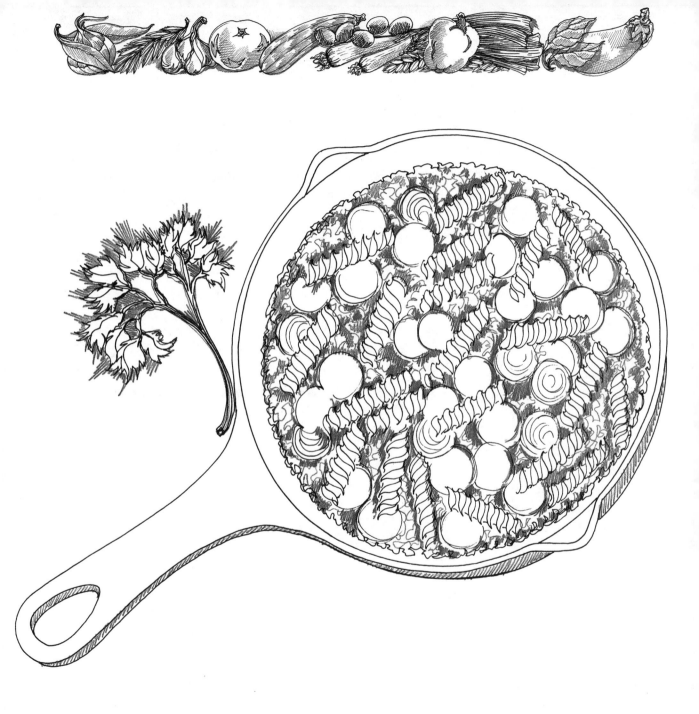

Roberta Wallace's Upside-Down Hamburger Pie

Kids will love this upside-down pie with the meat on the bottom and the rice on the top.

makes 6 servings

Crust:

2	heels of bread
1/3	cup tomato paste
1	pound lean ground beef
1/4	cup finely chopped onions
1/2	teaspoon salt
1/8	teaspoon dried oregano
	freshly ground black pepper

Filling:

1 1/2	cups uncooked minute rice
1	cup water
12	ounces tomato sauce
1	cup grated cheddar cheese
	salt and pepper to taste

Preheat the oven to 350°F. Process bread in the food processor until you have fine crumbs. Combine 1/2 cup of the bread crumbs with tomato paste, ground beef, onions, salt, oregano, and pepper. Mix thoroughly with a wooden spoon, then press into a 9-inch metal pie pan forming a "crust."

Pour the uncooked rice, water, tomato sauce, and half the cheese into the crust. Cover with aluminum foil and bake 25 minutes. Uncover, sprinkle with remaining cheese and bread crumbs, then bake, uncovered, until rice is tender, about 15 minutes more.

Let the pie stand 10 minutes or so before cutting into 6 wedges. This pie looks great served with a sprig of fresh parsley on the side.

Per serving: 453 calories, 25 g. fat, 101 mg. cholesterol, 1,233 mg. sodium

English Beef and Onion Dinner

Although this simmers almost half a day, it requires very little of the cook's time. Serve with boiled potatoes and thick slices of stewed tomatoes for a good dinner on a foggy, cold, English-style night.

makes 6 servings

1½	**pounds lean ground beef**
3	**pounds yellow onions, thinly sliced**
3	**cloves garlic, finely chopped**
1	**cup beef stock**
1	**bottle of dark beer**
1	**teaspoon thyme**
2	**ribs celery and leaves, finely chopped**
1	**teaspoon sugar**
1	**tablespoon apple-cider vinegar**

In a large stewpot, brown the meat, onions, and garlic until the beef loses its pinkish cast. Then lower the heat and add stock, beer, thyme, celery, sugar, and vinegar. Stir, then cover and simmer about 2 hours. Serve alongside boiled new potatoes.

Per serving: 385 calories, 19 g. fat, 92 mg. cholesterol, 101 mg. sodium

Stir-Fried Skillet Supper

Here's dinner in 15 minutes. Boil a pot of noodles, stir-fry the ground beef with green onions and mushrooms, and you have a healthy, easy meal in a hurry.

makes 4 servings

4	packets of ramen noodles
2	cloves garlic, coarsely chopped
1	bunch green onions with tops, sliced diagonally
1	cup sliced fresh button mushrooms
1	tablespoon sesame oil
1	pound lean ground beef
2	tablespoons rice vinegar
1	tablespoon each barbecue sauce and chili paste
	salt and freshly ground black pepper to taste

Cook the ramen noodles in a large pot of boiling, barely salted water, just until limp, about 3 minutes. Drain and reserve.

Meanwhile, in a wok over high heat, cook the garlic, onions, and mushrooms a minute or so in the oil. Add the ground beef and stir-fry just until the meat loses its pink cast. Add vinegar and cook 30 seconds more.

Stir in the barbecue sauce, chili paste, salt, and pepper.

Serve the stir-fry on a bed of ramen noodles.

Per serving: 412 calories, 19 g. fat, 92 mg. cholesterol, 429 mg. sodium

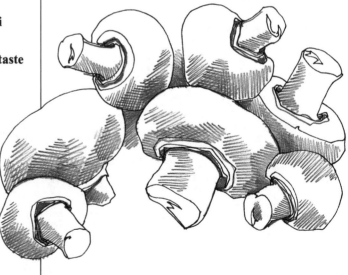

Joe's Sloppy Joes

Serve these family favorites on hot Kaiser rolls with plenty of shredded iceberg lettuce on top. It's dinner in 30 minutes and with only one pan to wash. That's the main reason Joe likes it.

makes 4 servings

1	**pound lean ground beef**
2	**medium onions, finely chopped**
1	**green or yellow bell pepper, seeded and finely chopped**
6	**large cloves garlic, finely chopped**
2	**tablespoons chili powder**
1	**can (28 ounces) Italian plum tomatoes, drained and chopped, juice reserved**
½	**cup chili sauce**
½	**cup canned beef broth**
2	**teaspoons red-wine vinegar**
2	**teaspoons Worcestershire sauce**
	salt and freshly ground black pepper to taste

Crumble beef into the bottom of a black cast-iron Dutch oven and brown it over medium-high heat until it begins to lose its pink color, about 5 minutes.

Reduce the heat to medium, and add—one item at a time—the onions, peppers, and garlic. Take your time, let this mixture cook down, about 15 minutes. Mix in the chili powder and continue cooking 2 minutes. Add tomatoes, chili sauce, broth, vinegar, Worcestershire sauce, and parsley. Cook until the vegetables are tender and the mixture is thick. Stir frequently. If the mixture seems too thick and threatens to stick to the bottom, add a little tomato juice or beef broth that you've reserved. Season with salt and pepper, then spoon onto hot Kaiser rolls. Top with generous handfuls of shredded iceberg lettuce and serve open-faced. A kosher pickle and a handful of potato chips completes this dinner.

Per serving: 392 calories, 20 g. fat, 92 mg. cholesterol, 412 mg. sodium

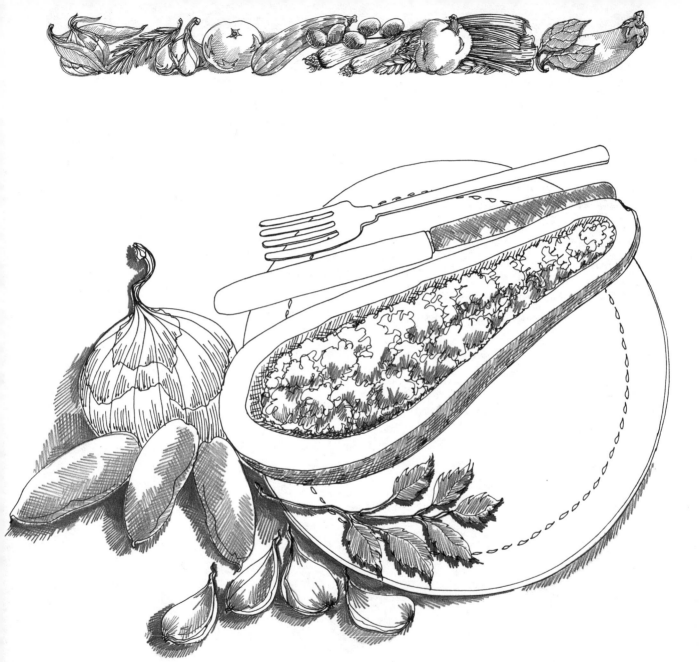

Squash Burglar

When August comes and the zucchinis blow up into boats, about the only thing you can do with them, besides sneak them onto the neighbor's porch in the dead of night, is use them as a home for savory fillings. Combine a big squash with ground beef, and you'll get a succulent late-summer dinner.

Feel free to substitute enormous Pattypan squashes, or small pumpkins, for the big zuke. You can, of course, divide the filling among single serving–sized squashes and make a handsome plate service of this one-dish dinner.

makes 6 servings

1	**summer squash (3 to 4 pounds)**
2	**tablespoons olive oil**
1	**large yellow onion, coarsely chopped**
4	**cloves garlic, finely chopped**
½	**pound lean ground beef**
½	**pound ground pork**
2	**cups chopped plum tomatoes**
2	**cups bread crumbs**
½	**cup finely chopped Italian parsley**
1	**teaspoon dried oregano**
	salt and freshly ground black and red pepper to taste
¾	**cup freshly grated Parmesan cheese**

Preheat the oven to 350°F. Cut the squash in two pieces. Scoop out the seeds and pith, leaving a ½-inch-thick shell. Place the squash halves on a cookie sheet and parbake them 15 minutes while you're preparing the filling.

In a large skillet, heat the oil over medium-high heat, then sauté the onions and garlic until the onions are beginning to brown. Crumble in the ground meats and continue cooking until the meat has lost its pink cast.

Stir in the tomatoes, turn the heat down to medium, and simmer until the tomatoes are tender and the liquid has almost all evaporated, about 15 minutes. Remove from the heat and stir in the bread crumbs, parsley, oregano, salt, and peppers.

Remove the squash from the oven and pat out any accumulated juices from the cavity with a paper towel. Scoop the filling into the squash halves, top with Parmesan, and pop it back in the oven.

Bake 30 minutes, then remove from the oven and let it stand 5 minutes before serving. Slice thick slices of meat and squash for each serving.

Per serving: 607 calories, 30 g. fat, 95 mg. cholesterol, 2,097 mg. sodium

Hamburger Tostadas With Fresh Corn Salsa

To present this dish, mound crisp corn tortillas with a base of avocado and a layer of crisp cooked hamburger, then top with fresh corn salsa. Garnish the plates with whole fresh jalapeños and sprigs of cilantro. It looks good and it tastes good.

makes 6 servings

1½	pounds lean ground beef
2	large yellow onions, finely chopped
2	tablespoons white-wine vinegar
2	cloves garlic, pressed
	salt and freshly ground black pepper to taste
	about 2 tablespoons vegetable oil or lard
4	ears of corn
2	large beefsteak tomatoes, finely chopped
1	small purple onion, finely chopped
2 or 3	jalapeño peppers
½	cup fresh chopped cilantro leaves
¼	cup fresh lime juice
2	large Haas avocados
8	7-inch corn tortillas or flat prepared tostada shells
	cilantro sprigs

In a large skillet, over medium-high heat, sauté the meat until it begins to lose its pinkish cast. Then stir in half the onions and continue to cook until the onions begin to brown. Add vinegar and garlic and continue to cook for 2 minutes. Season with salt and pepper, cover, and set aside.

Meanwhile, cook the corn in the husks in the microwave set at 100 percent (HIGH) for 15 minutes, or in a cauldron of boiling water for 3 minutes. Shuck the corn, then cut the kernels from the cob, using a sharp knife and holding the ear of corn over a bowl. Using the back of the knife, scrape the corn cob to release all the corn milk into the bowl.

Add the tomatoes, onions, jalapeños, cilantro, and 2 tablespoons of the lime juice to the corn kernels. Stir in the oil and salt, and stir until mixture is well blended. Cover and set aside at least 30 minutes to allow the flavors to marry.

Just before serving, reheat the meat over low heat. Peel and mash the avocados with remaining 2 tablespoons lime juice and salt.

In a medium skillet, fry corn tortillas in a thin layer of oil until crisp. (You can skip this step if you bought crisp fried corn tortillas to begin with.)

To assemble, spread a layer of avocado, then a layer of ground meat, then spoon salsa on top and serve. Garnish each serving with a jalapeño and a sprig of cilantro.

Per serving: 430 calories, 12 g. fat, 89 mg. cholesterol, 910 mg. sodium

Gordon Murray's Curry in a Hurry

When Gordon's in a hurry, he makes perfect rice in the microwave, stir-fries this hamburger curry in a skillet, and serves condiments from what's on hand in the pantry: raisins, peanuts, scallions and tops, hard-cooked eggs, tomato wedges, mint leaves, green peas, cucumbers. It's too easy.

makes 4 servings

Rice:
2	cups boiling water
1	cup basmati or Texmati rice
½	teaspoon salt

Curried Meat (Keema):
1	tablespoon cooking oil
2	large onions, minced
4	cloves garlic, minced
½	cup fresh bread crumbs
1	jalapeño or hot green chile, seeded and minced
⅛	teaspoon cinnamon
⅛	teaspoon cloves
1	egg white, whisked until foamy
¾	pound lean ground beef
	juice of one half a lemon
	salt and pepper to taste
¼	cup fresh or 2 tablespoons dried cilantro leaves

Sauce:
2	tablespoons margarine or butter
2	tablespoons flour
1	tablespoon (or to taste) curry powder
1½	cups chicken broth
1	small can (5.33 ounces) evaporated milk or coconut milk
	salt and red pepper to taste

First cook the rice. Bring water to a boil (in microwave set at 100 percent [HIGH] for 6 minutes), then dump in the rice and salt, cover, and microwave at 100 percent [HIGH] for 15 minutes. (Alternately, cook rice as directed on the box.)

To prepare meat, preheat a large skillet, add oil, then stir-fry the onions and garlic until limp and beginning to brown. Meanwhile, toss together the bread crumbs, chilies, cinnamon, cloves, egg white, and ground beef. Add to the skillet and stir-fry with the onions and garlic. Season with lemon juice, salt, pepper, and cilantro. Set aside.

While the meat is cooking, make the sauce by stirring the margarine or butter and flour in a medium saucepan until it's golden, then stir in curry powder and cook another minute or so, stirring. Stir in chicken broth and bring to a boil, stirring. Add milk. Boil until the sauce is thick and smooth. Taste and adjust seasonings with salt and red pepper.

To serve, make a layer of rice on a flat platter, pour the meat in the middle, and top with the sauce. Serve condiments on the side.

Per serving: 529 calories, 25 g. fat, 141 mg. cholesterol, 1,317 mg. sodium

You can make the meat mixture and the sauce ahead and refrigerate for 3 days, or you may freeze meat and sauce for up to 3 months. Then, just cook a pot of rice and prepare as directed.

Kat's Hamburger Moussaka

Use ground beef or lamb for this dish. Accompany with a pot of rice and a simple salad of bitter greens.

makes 6 servings

1	**pound lean ground beef or ground lamb**
3	**large yellow onions, coarsely chopped**
6	**cloves garlic, coarsely chopped**
1	**can (28 ounces) tomatoes (with juice)**
1	**teaspoon cinnamon**
	salt and freshly ground black pepper to taste

In a hot, dry, 10-inch skillet, brown the meat along with the onions and garlic over medium-high heat. Keep stirring the onions and garlic in and around the meat so that the onions will caramelize. Add a couple tablespoons of water to keep it from sticking; cover and steam a minute or two. This entire browning process should take about 10 minutes.

Add tomatoes and juice, cinnamon, salt, and pepper, then reduce heat and simmer, uncovered, for about 1 hour.

Meanwhile, make a pot of perfect rice (see page 79). Serve over rice with a green salad and a loaf of French bread and you're set.

Per serving: 215 calories, 12 g. fat, 61 mg. cholesterol, 226 mg. sodium

Navy Beans and Homemade Sausage Casserole

Begin with dried beans or canned, make your own impromptu sausage, and serve alongside applesauce and brown bread for a comfortable mid-winter meal.

makes 6 servings

4	cups cooked navy beans
1	pound lean ground beef
½	pound ground pork
1	medium onion, minced
1	clove garlic, minced
1	tablespoon sugar
3	tablespoons chili powder
1	teaspoon dried or 1 tablespoon fresh oregano
¼	teaspoon ground cloves
¼	teaspoon ground cumin
3	tablespoons red-wine vinegar
1	bell pepper, seeded and cut into rings

Heat the cooked beans in a casserole dish in a 350°F oven.

Meanwhile, mix the beef, pork, onions, garlic, sugar, chili powder, oregano, cloves, cumin, and vinegar. Squish it together with your hands.

Fry the meat mixture in a skillet over medium-high heat. Drain and sprinkle on top of the beans in the casserole dish. Top with pepper rings and heat in oven for 15 minutes.

Serve hot in rimmed soup bowls. It's even better the second day.

Per serving: 554 calories, 25 g. fat, 101 mg. cholesterol, 177 mg. sodium

Chinese Dumplings

Traditionally served for Chinese New Year, these tasty dumplings are sure to cure the mid-winter blues. If you wish to really celebrate the Chinese New Year, clean the house thoroughly before the new year begins to expel evil influences that might hide there. Avoid sweeping floors on the first day of the year—you may sweep good luck out the door. Settle all your old debts.

Serve a midnight supper. Include noodles for long life, egg rolls for prosperity, vegetables for happiness, sticky rice for family unity, and Chinese dumplings for wealth.

makes about 30 tortellini-shaped dumplings

¾	pound lean ground beef
1	medium onion, quartered
1	large rib celery with leaves
1	knob of ginger, 1 inch long, peeled
½	teaspoon fennel seeds
¼	teaspoon coarsely ground black pepper
1	tablespoon oyster sauce
1	large egg
1	package (16 ounces) 3-inch-square wonton wrappers
1	tablespoon cornstarch dissolved in 2 tablespoons water
1⅓	cups water
½	cup rice-wine vinegar
½	teaspoon sugar
1	tablespoon reduced-sodium soy sauce

Place ground meat in a cold skillet, then turn the heat to medium-high. Finely chop the onion, celery, and ginger in the food processor using the steel blade, then add to the skillet, stirring.

Add fennel seeds, pepper, and oyster sauce and cook until the meat has lost its pink cast. Remove the meat mixture to a bowl to cool. Wipe out the skillet.

Whisk egg into the meat mixture. Lay the wrappers on a flat surface. Dab two edges of the wrapper with the cornstarch mixture to glue the edges together. Place a teaspoon of filling in the center of the wrapper, fold the wrapper diagonally into a triangle, pressing down on the edges to seal shut. Then with one hand, pull the end of a long side of the triangle and with your other hand, pull the end of the other long side and make the two ends overlap, then press them firmly together, making a tortellini shape.

Remove the triangular filled dumpling to a sheet of waxed paper lightly dusted with cornstarch. Repeat, until you have filled about 30 dumplings and used all the filling.

Preheat two large skillets over medium-high heat. Spray each skillet with vegetable nonstick spray, then place the dumplings in the skillets, sides not touching. Cook 1 minute or until the bottoms are begin-

ning to brown. Reduce heat to medium-low, add ⅔ cup water to each skillet, cover, and steam the dumplings for 10 minutes. Uncover and cook until remaining water evaporates.

Remove the dumplings to a warm dish. Mix vinegar, sugar, and soy sauce for a dipping sauce. The dumplings are best eaten hot, but they are also delicious cold.

Per serving: 420 calories, 11 g. fat, 75 mg. cholesterol, 990 mg. sodium

Chapter Four

THE TOP TWENTY CHILIS, SOUPS, AND STEWS

Ground beef can be used successfully in many chilis, soups, and stews. Recipes that might take a half a day if made with stew meat go together quickly using ground meats and will cook in much less time.

As with all soups and stews, you'll get the very best taste if you make the soup slowly: cook it, then cool it, covered, and reheat it. That's when you get the marriage of flavors that makes people come back for more.

Don't try to hurry the beginnings of soups by dumping all the ingredients into the pot at one time. If you sauté the vegetables and sear the ground beef, as described in the recipes, you'll get that luscious caramelization that will melt into the soup's liquid and make the flavor as complex as a fine perfume.

For recipes calling for meatballs in the stew, see the introduction to the meatball chapter (see page 110) for directions about forming meatballs.

To get the best taste out of any chili recipe, cook in a cast-iron Dutch oven. Some of the iron leaches out into the sauce and gives it the muscle to stand up and be counted. If any chili recipe isn't hot enough to suit you, toss in a spoonful of fresh salsa, or chop in additional jalapeños. If you get the chili made and discover it's *too hot,* tame the heat with a pinch of sugar or a shot of catsup, or quickly eat some hot buttered flour tortillas. Serve some iced tea in quarts.

Remember, chili is also delicious spooned over scrambled eggs, grits, spaghetti squash, or plain old spaghetti.

All of these chilis, soups, and stews freeze well. Whenever I make one of these recipes, I divide the leftovers among pint-sized freezer containers. Then, I have on hand a quick lunch for two, with no more work than thawing and heating the soup in the microwave—a home-cooked meal in five minutes flat.

Now that is what America loves, and that is your reward for taking the time and trouble to make a big pot of soup. Enjoy.

Desert Storm Chili

1st Place Winner, Hawaii, 1991 National Beef
Cook-off

Desert Finkelstein was a medical petty officer in
the navy sitting around bored in the desert during the
1990 Desert Storm action in the Middle East. He
invented this recipe out of a longing for his family
and the good times he'd had in Illinois making 20
gallons of chili at a time out in the backyard over a
propane burner. David was only home from the war
one week when he learned he'd won a chance to
make chili at the National Beef Cook-off.

makes 12 servings

8	ounces dried red kidney beans
4	ounces dried great Northern beans
1½	quarts water
1	pound lean ground beef
2	pounds boneless top sirloin steak, cut into ¾-inch pieces
1	tablespoon vegetable oil
1	large onion, chopped
2 or 3	cloves garlic, minced
1	cup each chopped leeks and chopped yellow or green bell peppers
1	tablespoon each paprika and crushed red pepper

2	teaspoons cayenne pepper
1½	teaspoons dried cumin (or to taste)
1	teaspoon dried oregano
	salt and freshly ground black pepper to taste
4	large tomatoes, peeled, seeded, and chopped
2	cans (14½ ounces each) beef stock
1	can (12 ounces) beer
	shredded cheddar cheese
	crusty French bread

In a large stew pot, cook the kidney and great Northern beans in boiling salted water about 10 minutes, then cover and set aside for 1½ hours.

Meanwhile, cook ground beef in a large skillet over medium-high heat until the beef is no longer pink, breaking up the meat with a large spoon. Remove the ground beef from the pan with a slotted spoon and reserve.

Brown the sirloin pieces in 2 batches in the same pan over medium-high heat. Remove the sirloin to the same bowl as the ground beef and reserve. Pour off the drippings.

Heat oil in the same skillet, then add onions and garlic. Cook until the onions are translucent, 3 to 5 minutes, stirring occasionally. Add leeks and peppers. Continue to cook until the vegetables are tender, 2 to 3 minutes.

Stir in the paprika, red pepper, cayenne, cumin, oregano, salt, and pepper. Cook 2 to 3 minutes, stirring. Add tomatoes, reduce the heat to medium-low, and cook until the tomatoes begin to break down, about 20 minutes. If necessary, add up to ½ cup beef broth to keep the tomato mixture from scorching.

Drain and rinse the beans. Combine beans, beef, tomato mixture, and remaining beef broth to a Dutch oven. Pour in the beer and stir. Bring to a boil, then reduce the heat to a simmer and cover and cook until the beans are tender, about 1½ hours. Stir frequently. Garnish chili with cheese. Serve with crusty bread.

Per serving: 512 calories, 23 g. fat, 102 mg. cholesterol, 217 mg. sodium

Coward's Chili

If somebody asks you to bring chili to the Boy Scout fund-raiser, here's one that will pass the tenderfoot test. If you'd like to pump up the flavor, just add cayenne pepper to taste for the grown-ups and garnish with jalapeño peppers.

For the kids, serve it plain in soup bowls with saltines.

makes 8 servings

1½	**pounds lean ground beef**
1	**medium yellow onion, coarsely chopped**
2	**medium bell peppers, seeded and chopped**
½	**teaspoon cumin**
2	**teaspoons chili powder (or to taste)**
1	**can (28 ounces) tomatoes (with juice)**
1	**can (6 ounces) tomato paste**
1	**can (15 ounces) tomato sauce**
2	**cans (15 ounces each) kidney beans (with liquid)**
	salt and freshly ground black pepper to taste

In the bottom of a large soup pot, brown the meat over medium-high heat with the onions and peppers. When the pinkish cast is gone from the meat and the onions are beginning to brown on the edges, stir in the cumin and chili powder. Cook and stir a couple of minutes, then add the tomato products. Add beans and liquid, taste, and adjust flavor with salt and pepper. Then turn heat down and simmer until tender and well blended, about 2 hours.

Per serving: 337 calories, 15 g. fat, 69 mg. cholesterol, 529 mg. sodium

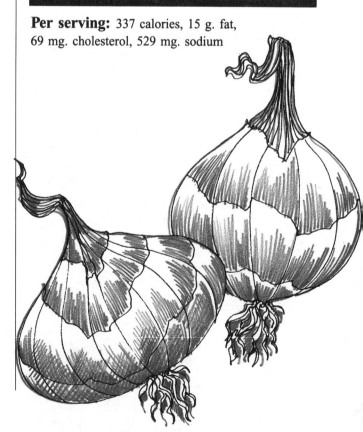

Farmer's Market Chili

Here's a good recipe to use lean hamburger meat. It's a dieter's delight, being low in both fats and cholesterol and high in the satisfaction quotient. It freezes well and is no trouble to make in a big pot.

makes 36 servings (18 pints)

1	**cup dry navy beans**
1	**cup dry red kidney beans**
1	**can (30 ounces) chili beans (with liquid)**
¼	**cup olive oil**
2	**eggplants, coarsely chopped**
2	**large yellow onions, coarsely chopped**
6	**cloves garlic, minced**
2	**medium zucchinis, coarsely chopped**
1	**large green or red bell pepper, seeded and diced**
2 or 3	**jalapeño peppers, seeded and minced**
3	**pounds Roma tomatoes, coarsely chopped (or 3 cans [16 ounces each], with juice)**
2	**tablespoons chili powder**
1	**tablespoon whole cumin seeds**
1	**teaspoon dried oregano**
	salt and freshly ground black pepper
1½	**pounds lean ground beef**
	plain nonfat yogurt or sour cream
	grated Longhorn or cheddar cheese
	chopped green onions and tops
	fresh cilantro leaves
	fresh minced tomatoes

Cover navy beans and kidney beans with 1 inch of salted water in a large saucepan and parboil, about 45 minutes. Then combine with chili beans and continue to cook.

Meanwhile, heat a large soup pot over medium-high heat, then add oil. Chop each vegetable (a food processor makes it easy) and add one at a time to the hot oil, beginning with eggplant, then onions, garlic, zucchini, peppers, jalapeños, and tomatoes. Take your time, giving each vegetable time to sauté. Stir, but keep the heat up so the vegetables begin to brown.

Once the vegetables have begun to cook down, about 30 minutes, season with chili powder, cumin, oregano, salt, and pepper. Add ground beef and cook until meat is no longer pink, then pour in all the beans.

Turn the heat down to medium-low and let the chili simmer, uncovered, for 2 to 3 hours, stirring occasionally. Add water as needed to maintain a soupy consistency.

Cover and let the chili stand until it reaches room temperature. Adjust seasonings with salt and pepper. You can reheat and serve it, or you can freeze it in pint-sized containers.

Serve each bowl with a dollop of yogurt or sour cream, and a sprinkling of cheese, green onions, cilantro and/or tomatoes.

Per serving: 85 calories, 5 g. fat, 15 mg. cholesterol, 54 mg. sodium

Beef Borscht

Eastern European in origin, this deep claret-colored soup is healthful, satisfying, and easy to make. Take your time at the beginning, allowing each vegetable to sauté before you add the next one. If you really wish to trim back on fats, use nonfat imitation sour cream on the top instead of the more traditional rich sour cream we all adore.

makes 16 to 20 servings

¾ pound lean ground beef
2 medium onions, finely chopped
3 large ribs celery, finely sliced
3 medium carrots, finely chopped
1 small head purple cabbage, finely chopped
1 can (15 ounces) sliced beets (with juice)
1 can (28 ounces) tomatoes (with juice)·
1 teaspoon sugar
   salt and freshly ground black pepper to taste
2 cans (15 ounces each) beef broth
   juice of half a lemon
   sour cream (optional)

In a large soup pot, brown the meat with the onions, celery, and carrots, adding the vegetables one at a time, taking your time.

Add cabbage, beets and juice, tomatoes and juice, sugar, salt, pepper, and broth. Squeeze in the lemon juice. Bring to a boil, cover, reduce heat, and simmer about 1½ hours. Taste and adjust seasonings. Serve in soup bowls with a dollop of sour cream atop, if desired.

Per serving: 74 calories, 3 g. fat, 16 mg. cholesterol, 131 mg. sodium

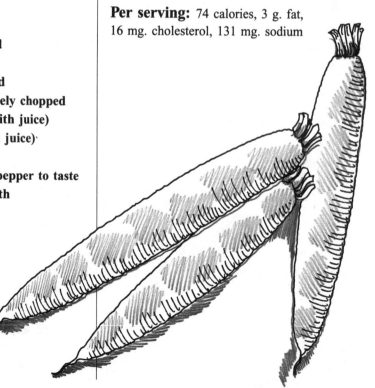

Fifties Retro Slumgullion

Beaver Cleaver's mother wasn't the only one to immortalize hamburger meat and macaroni. If you can use lean ground beef, you, too, can learn to love this skillet dinner that was the grandmother to hamburger and all its helpers.

makes 6 servings

1	**tablespoon olive oil**
2	**medium onions, diced**
1	**medium bell pepper, diced**
1	**cup uncooked elbow macaroni**
1½	**pounds lean ground beef**
1	**can (16 ounces) tomatoes (with juice)**
	salt and pepper to taste

In a large stew pot in hot oil, brown the onions, peppers, and macaroni. Stir until all the ingredients are coated with oil and the vegetables are beginning to brown on the edges.

Crumble the ground beef into the vegetables and brown. Add tomatoes and juice, plus a canful of water, and lower the heat to a simmer. Cover and cook until the macaroni is soft, about 35 minutes. Add water as necessary to keep it from sticking to the bottom.

When the macaroni is tender but not falling apart, season with salt and pepper and serve at once in soup bowls.

Per serving: 342 calories, 21 g. fat, 92 mg. cholesterol, 261 mg. sodium

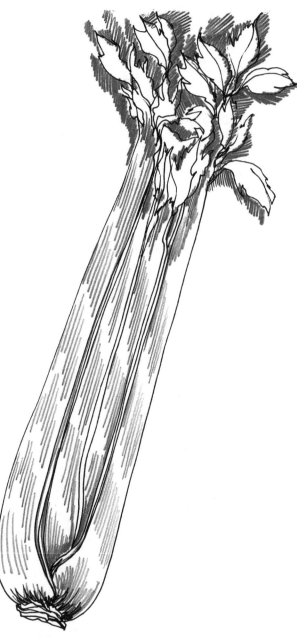

Sweet-and-Sour Cabbage Soup With Pumpernickel Croutons

This sweet-and-sour soup is complex and interesting, offering sweetness from molasses and a sour pucker from lemon juice. The herbs and spices give it a distinct Eastern European signature. Make or buy a loaf of black bread to accompany. This dinner's good, cheap, and memorable.

makes 8 to 10 servings

2	tablespoons vegetable oil
1	large onion, finely chopped
1	medium carrot, finely chopped
1	teaspoon sugar
1	pound lean ground beef
1	rib celery, finely chopped
1	head cabbage (1 pound), finely chopped
1	pound tomatoes, fresh or canned (with juice)
1	can (14½ ounces) beef broth
½	cup dark molasses
4	saltine crackers, crumbled
½	teaspoon ground ginger
¼	teaspoon ground cinnamon
¼	teaspoon ground cloves
½	teaspoon dried dillweed

1   teaspoon caraway seeds
     juice of 1 lemon
1   quart warm water
     salt and freshly ground black pepper to taste
     pumpernickel croutons (see recipe below)

In a large soup pot, heat oil over medium-high heat, then sauté onions and carrots until pearly and beginning to brown around the edges. Sprinkle with sugar and continue to caramelize, about 3 minutes. Add ground beef, then cook and stir until the pink color disappears.

Add celery and cabbage and continue to cook and stir until cabbage begins to brown on the edges. Add tomatoes and juice, broth, molasses, cracker crumbs, ginger, cinnamon, cloves, dill, and caraway seeds. Stir, then cook about 15 minutes.

Add lemon juice and water. Taste and adjust seasonings with salt and pepper. You can also add more sugar or some vinegar if you'd like to enhance the sweetness or sourness. Simmer the soup, uncovered, for an hour or so. Turn the heat off and set the soup pot in a pan of ice water to quickly chill it. Then cover and refrigerate. Reheat to serve.

Per serving: 266 calories, 12 g. fat, 41 mg. cholesterol, 226 mg. sodium

Pumpernickel Croutons

makes 2 cups croutons

4   slices pumpernickel bread
¼   cup margarine or butter
     freshly ground black pepper

Dry out bread in a 325°F oven until beginning to brown, about 15 minutes. Then cut it into ½-inch cubes. Toss with margarine or butter and pepper in a hot skillet until toasty brown.

Good and Cheap Tip

Little has changed since Marco Polo made his way trading spices. Spices are still as expensive as gold. You can save money by buying them in bulk at a natural food store, ethnic market, or local farmer's market. Buy a small amount, then store in recycled baby food or other small glass jars. Label and date the jars, then store in a cool, dark place.

Halloween Soup in a Pumpkin

Use a pumpkin as a soup tureen. As you serve each bowlful, scoop pumpkin flesh in with the soup. Garnish with a dollop of plain yogurt, then float a jalapeño ring or sprig of parsley on the top.

makes 8 servings

1	large pumpkin (about 12 inches tall)
2	cups milk
	salt and freshly ground black pepper to taste
1	medium onion, finely chopped
4	cloves garlic
2	tablespoons margarine or butter
1	pound lean ground beef
2	tablespoons unbleached white flour
2	medium tomatoes, chopped
2	cups roasted pumpkin flesh, cut into 2-inch chunks
1	tablespoon chili powder
¼	teaspoon cayenne pepper
¼	teaspoon dried oregano
3	cups beef broth
	sour cream or plain nonfat yogurt
	parsley and jalapeño peppers

To make a tureen from a pumpkin shell, choose one that is hard with no soft spots and as perfectly round as possible.

Preheat the oven to 350°F. Cut the top third off the pumpkin. Scrape out the seeds and fiber using a tablespoon. Reserve the seeds. Rinse both inside sections of the pumpkin with milk, then salt lightly and pepper generously. Replace the top, place the whole pumpkin on a cookie sheet, and place it on the bottom rack of the oven. Roast until tender, about 1 hour. Reserve the accumulated liquid in the bottom to pour into the soup; it's too good to waste. Scoop out the flesh to add to the soup.

In a large, stainless steel soup pot over medium-high heat, sauté onions and garlic in margarine or butter until the onions look pearly and begin to brown on the edges. Add ground beef and cook until pink has disappeared. Sprinkle with flour, then cook and stir until you have a golden roux, about 8 minutes.

Add tomatoes, pumpkin chunks, chili powder, cayenne, oregano, and broth. Boil gently over medium heat for about 15 minutes. Add 1 cup milk and adjust the seasonings with salt and pepper. Bring to a boil, then pour into the hot pumpkin-shell tureen to serve. Float sour cream or yogurt on top. Garnish with parsley and jalapeño peppers sliced crosswise into "flowers" and lengthwise into "stems."

Per serving: 219 calories, 14 g. fat, 58 mg. cholesterol, 233 mg. sodium

Meatball Minestrone

The classic Italian flavoring of nutmeg and meatballs makes this a soup to remember. Combine Italy's vegetable soup with the country's particular meatballs, dust the top of the soup with Parmesan, float a fresh basil leaf on top, and you know it has to be summer.

makes 8 servings

Meatballs:

½	pound ground veal
1	pound lean ground beef
½	cup milk
1	cup fresh bread crumbs
½	teaspoon nutmeg
2	tablespoons minced parsley
2	tablespoons minced onions
	salt and freshly ground black pepper to taste
¼	cup grated Parmesan cheese
2	tablespoons olive oil

Soup:

¼	cup olive oil
¼	cup butter
1	medium yellow onion, thinly sliced
2	medium carrots, peeled and diced
2	ribs celery and leaves, diced
3	medium potatoes, diced
1	can (15 ounces) Great Northern beans or 1½ cups cooked dried Cannellini or Great Northern beans
2	medium zucchini, diced
1	cup fresh or frozen green beans, cut in 2-inch pieces
4	cups shredded cabbage (Savoy's the best)
2	cans (15 ounces each) beef broth
2	cups dry red wine
1	can (28 ounces) stewed plum tomatoes (with juice)
1	cup uncooked rigatoni or other pasta
	salt and freshly ground black pepper
½	cup grated Parmesan cheese
	basil or parsley sprigs

Crumble the ground meats. Then pour in the milk and sprinkle with bread crumbs to soak up the moisture. Season with nutmeg, parsley, onions, salt, pepper, and Parmesan. Squish the mixture together with your hands, then divide into 24 equal-sized pieces, rolling each into a ball about the size of a walnut.

Fry the meatballs in a large skillet in oil until brown on all sides. Set aside.

Meanwhile, in a large soup pot, begin the soup by sautéing in oil and butter the onions, carrots, celery, and potatoes, until the onions are beginning to brown and the potatoes are opaque and beginning to brown. Take your time, it will take about 20 minutes.

Pour in the beans, zucchini, green beans, cabbage, and broth. Bring to a boil and add the wine. Turn heat down to a simmer and cook until the vegetables are tender and somewhat reduced, about 20 minutes more.

Add meatballs, tomatoes and juice, and the pasta and cook until al dente, about 10 minutes. Adjust seasonings with salt and pepper.

To serve, place 2 or 3 meatballs in the bottom of each soup bowl, fill the bowl with soup, and dust the top with Parmesan. Garnish with a sprig of fresh basil or parsley and serve.

Per serving: 603 calories, 32 g. fat, 106 mg. cholesterol, 1,060 mg. sodium

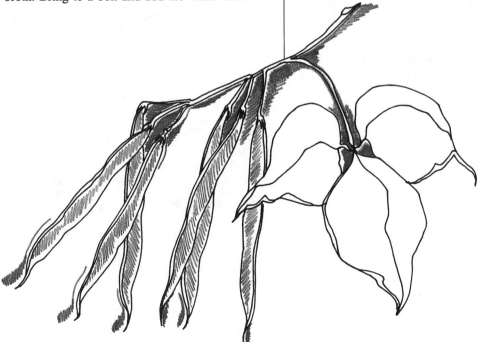

Laurie Howard's Cabbage-Patch Soup

Laurie makes a batch of cornbread to go with this soup, and her family calls it their favorite.

makes 6 servings

1	**pound lean ground beef**
½	**teaspoon chili powder**
1	**medium onion, sliced**
2	**cups shredded green cabbage**
½	**cup diagonally sliced celery**
2	**cups water**
1	**can (16 ounces) chili beans**
1	**can (16 ounces) Italian-style stewed tomatoes (with juice)**
	salt and freshly ground black pepper to taste
2	**cups hot mashed potatoes**

Brown the beef and chili powder in the bottom of a stew pot over medium-high heat. Add onions, cabbage, and celery and cook until the onions are translucent. Add water, cover, reduce the heat, and simmer 15 minutes. Add beans and tomatoes and juice and simmer an additional 15 minutes. Taste and adjust seasonings with salt and pepper.

Serve in wide-rimmed soup bowls with a scoop of mashed potatoes floating on top.

Per serving: 265 calories, 13 g. fat, 61 mg. cholesterol, 259 mg. sodium

Hearty Beef and Barley Soup

From Eastern Europe comes this version of a soup sure to stick to your ribs. Serve with black bread and butter.

makes 8 servings

1	**can (16 ounces) tomatoes (with juice)**
2	**quarts water**
1	**medium yellow onion, thinly sliced**
2	**ribs celery and leaves, diced**
¼	**cup parsley, finely chopped**
¾	**pound lean ground beef**
½	**cup barley**
½	**cup small dry lima beans**
1	**carrot, peeled and thinly sliced**
1	**pound fresh mushrooms, thinly sliced**
2	**teaspoons dried dillweed**
½	**teaspoon caraway seeds**
	salt and freshly ground black pepper to taste

In the bottom of a large soup pot, bring the tomatoes and juice to a boil over medium-high heat. Add water, onions, celery, parsley, ground beef, barley, and lima beans. Bring to a boil, then reduce the heat and simmer, uncovered, until the limas and barley are tender, about 1½ hours.

Add carrots, mushrooms, dill, and caraway seeds. Simmer until carrots are tender, about 30 minutes more. Adjust seasonings with salt and pepper and serve.

Per serving: 182 calories, 6 g. fat, 35 mg. cholesterol, 165 mg. sodium

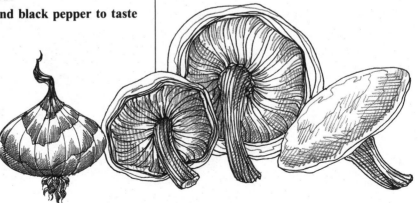

Spanish Rice Sopa Seca

In the first place, what Americans call Spanish rice is really from Mexico. In the second place, Mexicans call soups wet or dry. This dry soup makes a great one-skillet dinner for a family.

makes 4 servings

1	slice bacon, cut into 1-inch pieces
1	cup uncooked long-grain white rice
1	medium onion, coarsely chopped
1	pound lean ground beef
1	can (16 ounces) tomatoes (with juice)
2	cups tomato juice
1	cup water
½	teaspoon ground cloves
1	dried bay leaf, crushed
	salt and freshly ground black pepper to taste
1	cup fresh or frozen peas
2	scallions and tops, chopped

In a 12-inch skillet over medium-high heat, cook the bacon until crisp. Lift the bacon out of the skillet and reserve. Pour in the rice. Cook until the grains are beginning to brown.

Add the onions to the skillet; cook and stir until the onions are beginning to brown. Add ground beef to the skillet and cook until the beef has lost its pinkish cast.

Pour in the tomatoes and juice, tomato juice, water, cloves, bay leaf, salt, and pepper. Stir to mix thoroughly. Bring to a boil, then reduce the heat, cover, and cook until the rice is tender, about 15 minutes.

Stir in the peas. Cover and let it stand, off the heat, about 5 minutes. Serve in rimmed soup bowls, garnished with green onions.

Per serving: 436 calories, 23 g. fat, 98 mg. cholesterol, 831 mg. sodium

Porcupines in the Stew

Here's a good use for that leftover cooked rice sitting in the back of your refrigerator. Make porcupine meatballs, then float them in this simple stew for a quick, satisfying supper.

makes 6 servings

Stew:

1	**can (28 ounces) tomatoes (with juice)**
2	**cans (15 ounces each) tomato sauce**
1	**tablespoon chili powder**
1	**can (12 ounces) of beer**
¼	**teaspoon allspice**
1	**teaspoon Worcestershire sauce**
½	**teaspoon brown sugar**

Porcupine Meatballs:

1	**pound lean ground beef**
1	**cup cooked rice**
½	**cup each finely chopped onions, bell peppers, and celery**
2	**egg whites, whisked**
1	**teaspoon German-style whole-seed mustard**
	salt and freshly ground black pepper to taste
½	**cup parsley, finely cut with scissors**

In a stew pot, combine tomatoes and juice, tomato sauce, chili powder, beer, allspice, Worcestershire sauce, and brown sugar. Bring to a boil, then reduce heat and let it simmer while you make the meatballs.

Combine the ground beef, rice, onions, peppers, and celery. Add egg whites, mustard, salt, and pepper. Squish it together with your hands, then form meatballs about the size of golf balls. Drop the meatballs into the simmering stew.

Let the stew simmer until the meatballs are thoroughly cooked, about 40 minutes. Taste and adjust seasonings with salt and pepper. Serve in rimmed soup bowls, garnished with parsley.

Per serving: 383 calories, 13 g. fat, 61 mg. cholesterol, 924 mg. sodium

Midwestern Hamburger Stew

This wholesome one-dish dinner only calls for a side of cornbread and apple pie for dessert.

makes 6 servings

2	cans (15 ounces each) beef broth
1	medium carrot, peeled and cut into chunks
½	pound pearl onions
1	pound lean ground beef
¼	cup low-fat (2%) milk
¼	cup all-purpose flour
¼	teaspoon ground cloves
	salt and freshly ground black pepper to taste
1	tablespoon butter or margarine
12	small red potatoes (about 1½ pounds)
½	cup chopped fresh parsley

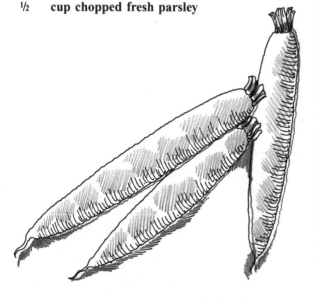

In a soup pot, bring the broth to a boil, adding the carrots and onions. Simmer, uncovered.

Meanwhile, form the ground beef into 12 equal-sized meatballs. Pour the milk into a bowl and dip each meatball into the milk. Reserve the leftover milk.

In a second bowl, combine the flour, cloves, salt, and pepper. Roll the meatballs in the flour mixture, then set aside for a few minutes. Save the flour.

Heat butter or margarine in a skillet and brown the meatballs on all sides. Add the potatoes and sauté 1 minute more. Pour into the soup pot and continue cooking.

Spoon out a little soup into the skillet and deglaze the pan, then pour the mixture back into the stew pot.

Stir the remaining milk and flour mixture together until it's free of lumps, then whisk it into the stew. Simmer, uncovered, until the stew is thick. Taste and adjust seasonings with salt and pepper. Garnish with parsley and serve.

Per serving: 344 calories, 15 g. fat, 68 mg. cholesterol, 256 mg. sodium

Beef Stew with Buttered Parsley Noodles

This stew is better the second day and freezes well. So make a big batch and divide it, and you'll have instant dinners on hand.

In a separate pot, cook a batch of egg noodles for the number of diners you have, toss with butter and parsley, then spoon the hot, savory stew on top.

makes 8 servings

2	pounds lean ground beef
	salt and pepper to taste
½	pound fresh mushrooms, sliced
3	large yellow onions, coarsely chopped
4	cloves garlic, finely chopped
2	teaspoons dried dillweed
½	teaspoon dried basil leaves
½	teaspoon dried thyme leaves
½	teaspoon dried savory leaves
1	dried bay leaf, crushed
2	cans (14½ ounces each) beef broth
1	pint water
1	pound carrots, peeled and cut into chunks
8	ounces uncooked egg noodles
½	cup fresh parsley, finely cut with scissors
1	tablespoon butter

In the bottom of a stew pot over medium-high heat, brown the ground beef along with salt, pepper, mushrooms, onions, and garlic. Add dill, basil, thyme, savory, and bay leaf and continue cooking until meat is no longer pinkish and the onions are beginning to brown on the edges.

Add the broth, water, and carrots. Cover and simmer until the carrots are tender, about 20 minutes. Taste and adjust seasonings.

Cook the noodles in a separate pan following package directions. Toss drained noodles with parsley and butter.

Serve stew over the buttered parsley noodles.

Per serving: 341 calories, 20 g. fat, 96 mg. cholesterol, 246 mg. sodium

Eggplant and Okra Stew

Make a pot of rice to go under this stew, and serve it alongside some yogurt spiked with raisins and a loaf of crusty French bread.

makes 6 servings

1	medium eggplant, unpeeled
	salt and freshly ground black pepper to taste
2	cups small whole okra
1	medium onion, sliced
1	cup parsley, finely cut with scissors
4	cloves garlic, finely sliced
2	tablespoons olive oil
1	pound lean ground beef
1	cup dry white wine
1	can (14½ ounces) beef broth

Cut the eggplant into 6 thick slices. Salt well and let it stand in a colander to draw out juices for 20 minutes or so.

Meanwhile, in a large stew pot, brown the okra, onions, parsley, and garlic in half the oil over medium-high heat until the onions are beginning to turn brown around the edges.

Add ground beef to the onion mixture and brown the meat. Pour in the wine and broth; season with salt and pepper. Turn the heat down to a simmer and cook gently about 30 minutes, stirring from time to time.

Rinse and dry the eggplant pieces, then brown them in a barely oiled large skillet. Add them to the stew, cover, and simmer until the eggplant is cooked through, about 1 hour more.

Taste and adjust seasoning, then serve over rice.

Per serving: 305 calories, 17 g. fat, 61 mg. cholesterol, 228 mg. sodium

Meatball Stew in Red Wine

Here's a French stew made practical by using low-cost ground beef instead of high-priced sirloin. Learn the old trick of using uncooked spaghetti to fasten the bacon around the meatball and you won't have to fish out toothpicks before serving.

makes 8 servings

6	strips of thinly-sliced, low-salt bacon, cut into 2-inch pieces
2	pounds lean ground beef
1	slice French bread
2	tablespoons milk
	salt and pepper to taste
	pieces of uncooked spaghetti
½	pound small boiling onions
1	pound small red potatoes
2	tablespoons unbleached white flour
1½	cups dry red wine
3	tablespoons brandy
1	medium onion
2	whole cloves
4	cloves garlic, pressed
¼	teaspoon dried marjoram
¼	teaspoon dried thyme
	zest of 1 orange
2	cups beef broth
½	pound fresh mushrooms
2	tablespoons margarine or butter
	finely chopped parsley

Lay bacon strips out, 1 layer deep on the counter top. Combine ground beef with bread, milk, salt, and pepper. Mix thoroughly. Divide the meat into 36 equal-sized balls and lay on bacon strips. Pull strips up to make a girdle and fasten to each meatball with a piece of dry spaghetti, leaving a ½-inch piece of pasta sticking out on each side.

Place meatballs in a dry, cold, 12-inch skillet, then heat over medium-high heat. Cook until meat is cooked through and brown on all sides, gently shaking the pan from time to time.

Transfer the meatballs to a 3-quart casserole dish. Add onions and potatoes to the skillet with meat drippings and brown, then lift these vegetables to the casserole dish.

Sprinkle flour over the meat drippings in the skillet and make a roux. Stir in wine and brandy. Stud the onion with cloves, then add it, along with the garlic, marjoram, thyme, orange zest, and broth, to the skillet. Bring to a boil, stirring. Adjust seasonings with salt and pepper, then pour into the casserole. Cover the casserole dish and place in a 325°F oven for 45 minutes.

Meanwhile, sauté the mushrooms in margarine or butter in the skillet, then stir them into the casserole 10 minutes before serving. Sprinkle with parsley and serve immediately.

Per serving: 527 calories, 31 g. fat, 111 mg. cholesterol, 600 mg. sodium

Beef Stew With Walnuts

Although this is a lot of stew, it's even better the second day, so make a big batch and eat it 2 days in a row. Or freeze what you don't eat the first day and warm it in the microwave later.

makes 8 servings

2	**pounds lean ground beef**
2	**tablespoons olive oil**
2	**tablespoons butter**
12	**small white boiling onions**
1	**tablespoon flour**
1	**cup dry red wine**
1	**cup beef stock**
1	**bay leaf**
1	**sprig fresh parsley**
1	**teaspoon dried thyme**
1	**clove garlic, minced**
	salt and pepper to taste
1	**bunch celery and tops, cut into thick slices**
¾	**cup walnut pieces**
	zest and juice of 1 orange

In a large soup pot, brown the beef in half the oil and half the butter. Add onions and continue to brown. Stir in the flour and make a roux. Add wine, stock, bay leaf, parsley, thyme, garlic, salt, and pepper.

Turn the heat to a simmer, cover, and cook for about an hour, stirring occasionally.

Meanwhile, in a large skillet, sauté the celery in the remaining oil and butter. Shake walnuts into the skillet when the celery has browned, and cook until the walnuts are crisp. Add to the stew. Stir in orange juice and zest and serve. Add boiled new potatoes or rice, if you like.

Per serving: 511 calories, 38 g. fat, 100 mg. cholesterol, 262 mg. sodium

Hamburger Chowder

Serve with saltine crackers and winter fruit for a complete, easy, mid-winter supper.

makes 8 servings

4	slices bacon, cut into 1-inch pieces
1	tablespoon butter or margarine
3	large yellow onions, thinly sliced
4	ribs celery, cut into ¼-inch pieces
½	teaspoon sugar
1	pound lean ground beef
1	quart water
4	medium russet potatoes (about 2 pounds), peeled and cut into ½-inch cubes
4	peppercorns
2	cups fresh or frozen corn kernels
	salt to taste

In the bottom of a soup pot over medium-high heat, brown the bacon, then lift out and reserve. Add butter or margarine, onions, and celery. Sprinkle with sugar. Cook and stir until the onions are beginning to brown on the edges. Add the ground beef and cook until the meat loses its pinkish cast.

Pour in the water and add potatoes and peppercorns. Turn the heat down and simmer until the potatoes are tender, about 20 minutes. Add the bacon, corn, and salt. Cover and let it stand until serving time. Reheat and serve in rimmed soup bowls.

Per serving: 229 calories, 18 g. fat, 62 mg. cholesterol, 422 mg. sodium

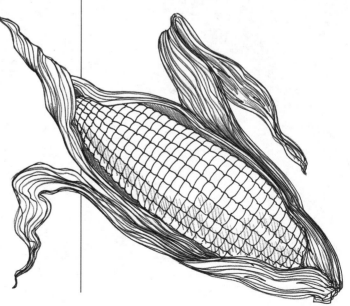

French Meatball Stew

The parsimonious French, known for saving even the most ignoble scraps when butchering, make a country stew from scraps of meat ground fine enough to make a paste. We use the leanest ground beef and find the results to be exquisite. Offer a couple of hot baguettes, candlelight, and the simplest salad of torn Romaine tossed in a vinaigrette. *Vive la France!*

serves 8

1	**pound lean ground beef**
1	**cup instant oatmeal**
	salt and freshly ground black pepper to taste
2	**tablespoons vegetable oil**
1	**bottle dry red wine or 4 cups water**
2	**cans (15 ounces each) beef stock**
2	**bay leaves**
1	**prepared bouquet garni**
½	**teaspoon dried thyme**
12	**small boiling onions**
1	**large head garlic, cloves separated but unpeeled**
4	**medium carrots, peeled and cut into ½-inch-thick coins**
4	**leeks, trimmed leaving 1 inch of green, then split vertically into 2 parts**
2	**cups button mushrooms**
	zest of 1 orange
12	**medium red potatoes**

Combine the meat with the oatmeal, season to taste with salt and pepper, then form into 16 equal-sized meatballs.

Heat a 10-inch skillet over medium-high heat, then add oil. Brown the meatballs all over until cooked through, shaking the pan from time to time to turn them.

Pour wine or water and stock into a soup pot, season with bay leaves, bouquet garni, and thyme and bring to a simmer.

Transfer the meatballs to the simmering stock. Then, in order, one at a time—onions, garlic, carrots, leeks, and mushrooms—sauté the vegetables in the skillet, adding each vegetable to the simmering stock as it begins to brown around the edges.

Finally, season the soup with orange zest, salt, and pepper and simmer for about an hour.

About 30 minutes before serving, sauté the potatoes in the skillet with remaining pan drippings, then add ½ cup of the soup stock, cover, and cook the potatoes until tender.

Just before serving, fish out and discard the bay leaves and bouquet garni. To serve, place 2 cooked potatoes in a soup bowl and top with stew. This stew is even better the second day, if you can leave enough for a free lunch for yourself later.

Per serving: 345 calories, 13 g. fat, 46 mg. cholesterol, 349 mg. sodium

Chapter Five

THE TOP TWENTY MEATBALLS

In this chapter you'll find meatballs of all sizes and originating from many different countries. Everything from pop-into-your-mouth bites up to baseball-sized meatballs are included here.

There are various ways to form meatballs. For my money, the best way is to get in with both hands and go at it. Take your rings off, plunge your hands into the meat mixture, squish it all together to mix thoroughly, then pinch off a bit and roll it between the palms of your hands.

Lay the formed meatballs out on a piece of waxed paper until you have them all formed. If you see one or two that look terribly outsized, reroll them.

If a recipe calls for, say, sixteen equal-sized meatballs I usually begin by dividing the meat in half, then in quarters, then each quarter into quarters. That way I have sixteen roughly equal parts. Then I start to roll.

I've seen experts in commercial kitchens rolling meatballs between two silver spoons by first dipping the spoons in cold water, then scooping up a mixture with one spoon, and forming it with the other. Frankly, when I tried this at home, it

was sort of like using chopsticks for the very first time. Practice—it must take practice.

I'll stick to hands, thank you. I like the feel of the food in my hands. I like to take a deep whiff of the aroma. I like the idea that the meatballs don't look like something kicked out by a computer-driven machine. So what if some are larger than others? So what if they're only roughly globular in shape? This way, my family knows I loved them enough to make dinner with my own two hands. I think that counts for something in this overly mechanized world we live in. Don't you?

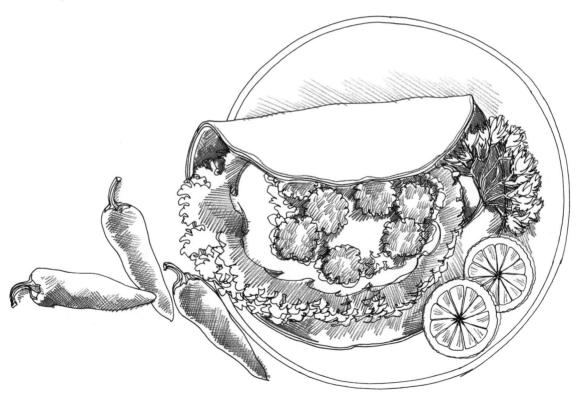

Orange Beef Meatballs and Broccoli

Here's an oriental-style meatball dish, bright with orange zest, red bell peppers, and dazzling green broccoli.

makes 4 servings

Meatballs:

3/4	**pound lean ground beef**
2	**cups hot cooked rice**
4	**teaspoons low-sodium soy sauce**
2	**teaspoons finely shredded fresh ginger**
1	**teaspoon orange zest**
1	**tablespoon peanut oil**
2	**cups broccoli florets**
1	**red bell pepper, seeded and cut into short, thin strips**
1/2	**teaspoon sugar**
1	**tablespoon water**

Sauce:

1/3	**cup orange juice**
2	**teaspoons cornstarch**
3	**scallions with tops, diagonally cut into 1-inch pieces**
	sliced almonds

Combine meat with 1/4 cup rice, soy sauce, ginger, and orange zest, then form into walnut-sized meatballs.

In a wok or large skillet, heat oil over medium-high heat, then cook meatballs until brown and done on all sides. Lift from the skillet to a warmed tray and reserve.

Add broccoli, peppers, and sugar to the skillet. Reduce the heat and add water, then cover and cook until broccoli is crisp-tender, about 3 minutes.

Combine orange juice and cornstarch. Add to the skillet along with the meatballs and onions. Cook and stir until the sauce is thick and clear, about 1 minute.

Serve over remaining rice and sprinkle with almonds.

Per serving: 488 calories, 19 g. fat, 92 mg. cholesterol, 1,382 mg. sodium

Cranberry Meatballs

For a festive dish to serve during the fall holidays, try this bright and tasty meatball dish. Serve with potato pancakes flecked with parsley.

makes 6 servings

Meatballs:

1½	pounds lean ground beef
¾	cup tomato juice
2	slices white bread
	salt and pepper to taste
1	tablespoon Worcestershire sauce
1	tablespoon minced fresh parsley
1	egg white, whisked

Sauce:

1	can (1 pound) whole cranberry sauce
1	tablespoon lemon juice
⅓	cup packed dark brown sugar

Mix ground beef with tomato juice and bread. Season with salt, pepper, Worcestershire sauce, and parsley, then whisk in the egg white. Form into walnut-sized balls and cook in a hot, dry skillet until evenly browned on all sides.

Meanwhile, make the sauce by whisking together the cranberry sauce, lemon juice, and brown sugar. Pour the sauce over the meatballs, lower the heat, cover, and simmer 30 minutes.

Serve with potato pancakes.

Per serving: 451 calories, 19 g. fat, 92 mg. cholesterol, 460 mg. sodium

Russian Meatballs

Serve these walnut-sized meatballs over parsley noodles with the sour cream sauce. Present it with red cabbage and a loaf of black bread, and it's dinner.

makes 50 meatballs, enough for 8 to 10 servings

Meatballs:

2	**pounds lean ground beef**
1	**medium onion, minced**
½	**teaspoon caraway seeds**
	salt and pepper to taste
2	**eggs, whisked**
¼	**cup vegetable oil or shortening**

Sauce:

¼	**cup unbleached white flour**
1¼	**cups water**
1	**cup sour cream or plain nonfat yogurt**
	juice and zest of ½ lemon
1	**teaspoon Worcestershire sauce**
1	**tablespoon chopped parsley**
	paprika

Preheat the oven to 350°F. Combine meat, onions, caraway seeds, salt, pepper, and eggs. Mix lightly with a fork, then, using 2 tablespoons, form into 1½-inch meatballs. Cover and set aside.

Heat oil or shortening in a large skillet over medium-high heat, then brown the meatballs, a few at a time. Remove them to a 13 × 9 × 2½-inch glass baking dish.

Add flour to remaining oil in the skillet and stir to make a roux. Add water, then cook and stir until thickened. Add sour cream or yogurt, lemon juice and zest, Worcestershire sauce, parsley, and paprika. Heat, but don't let it boil. Taste and adjust seasonings with additional salt and pepper.

Pour the sauce over the meatballs then bake, uncovered, for 20 minutes. Serve at once over parsley noodles or rice.

Per serving: 379 calories, 27 g. fat, 153 mg. cholesterol, 223 mg. sodium

Italian Meatballs and Spaghetti in Fresh Tomato Sauce

The very best tomato sauce begins with fresh Roma (plum) tomatoes and can only be made in the summer, when plum tomatoes are readily available. Should you have access to yellow plum tomatoes, you can make a gorgeous yellow sauce that surprises everyone.

makes 6 servings

Meatballs:

1	pound lean ground beef
½	pound ground veal
¼	cup minced onions
1	cup fresh bread crumbs
½	cup milk
¾	teaspoon nutmeg
¼	cup finely cut fresh parsley
¼	cup grated Parmesan cheese
¼	cup crushed red-pepper flakes
	salt and pepper to taste
¼	cup olive oil

Sauce:

¼	cup olive oil
2	medium yellow onions, finely chopped
6	cloves garlic, finely chopped
2	pounds fresh Roma tomatoes, finely chopped
1	can (6 ounces) tomato paste
2	tablespoons minced fresh basil
½	teaspoon dried oregano
2	cups water
	salt and freshly ground black pepper to taste
1	pound uncooked spaghetti or linguini
½	cup finely chopped Italian-style parsley

To make meatballs, crumble ground meats in a large mixing bowl. Add onions, bread crumbs, milk, nutmeg, parsley, Parmesan, red-pepper flakes, salt, and pepper. Squish ingredients together with your hands and form mixture into 36 meatballs. Brown on all sides in oil in a large skillet. Reserve.

To make the sauce, heat oil in a soup pot, then sauté the onions and garlic until the onions begin to turn golden. Add tomatoes. Cook and stir 5 minutes. Add tomato paste, basil, oregano, and water. Stir to mix. Raise to a boil, then lower the heat and simmer 20 minutes. Taste and adjust seasoning with salt and pepper.

Slip the cooked meatballs into the sauce and cook an additional 15 minutes while you boil up a pot of spaghetti following package directions.

Serve meatballs and sauce over cooked and drained spaghetti. Stir parsley into the meatballs and spaghetti just before serving. Dust with Parmesan.

Per serving: 620 calories, 36 g. fat, 85 mg. cholesterol, 910 mg. sodium

Moroccan Meatballs (kofta)

Serve these meatballs on a bed of couscous and add a sprig of mint for garnish. Side dishes of currants, chopped scallions and tops, and crystallized ginger would be nice.

makes 4 servings

Meatballs:
1	**pound lean ground beef**
½	**pound ground lamb**
½	**teaspoon cumin**
3	**cloves garlic**
¼	**cup fresh bread crumbs**
2	**egg whites, whisked until foamy**
	salt and red and black peppers to taste

Sauce:
¼	**cup olive oil**
1	**teaspoon cumin**
1	**teaspoon Hungarian paprika**
¼	**teaspoon crushed red pepper flakes**
½	**cup water**
	juice and zest of 1 lemon
	salt and freshly ground black pepper to taste

Crumble ground meats into a large mixing bowl. Add cumin, garlic, bread crumbs, egg whites, salt, and peppers. Squish ingredients together with your hands, then form mixture into 24 equal-sized meatballs. Cover and refrigerate.

In a large saucepan, combine oil, cumin, paprika, crushed red pepper flakes, water, and lemon juice and zest, and simmer 10 minutes. Taste and adjust seasonings with salt and pepper.

Add uncooked meatballs to the sauce, cover, and simmer until the meatballs are cooked, about 40 minutes. Serve meatballs and sauce on a bed of couscous.

Per serving: 639 calories, 49 g. fat, 92 mg. cholesterol, 928 mg. sodium

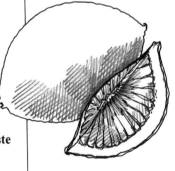
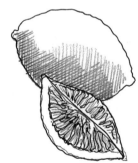

Swedish Meatballs

Ideal for a party chafing dish, these make way for other more labor-intensive tasks that await you, since they're baked, not fried.

makes 5 dozen small meatballs

Meatballs:

1	**pound ground beef**
½	**pound ground pork**
1	**cup dry bread crumbs**
2	**egg whites, whisked until foamy**
½	**cup low-fat (2%) milk**

Sauce:

½	**cup firmly packed brown sugar**
¼	**cup water**
¼	**cup apple-cider vinegar**
½	**teaspoon dry mustard**
½	**cup fresh parsley, finely cut with scissors**

Preheat oven to 325°F. Crumble the ground meats and add bread crumbs, egg whites, and milk. Squish together with your hands and form into walnut-sized meatballs. Place the meatballs 1 layer deep in an 11 × 5 × 2-inch baking dish.

To make the sauce, whisk together brown sugar, water, vinegar, and mustard. Pour over the meatballs, then bake for about 1 hour, basting occasionally.

Sprinkle with parsley just before serving. Serve hot from a chafing dish, with toothpicks for spears.

Per meatball: 38 calories, 2 g. fat, 7 mg. cholesterol, 18 mg. sodium
Sauce, per tablespoon: 10 calories, 0 g. fat, 0 mg. cholesterol, 2 mg. sodium

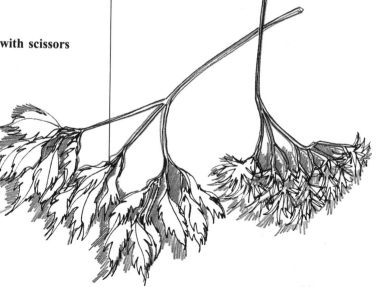

Hawaiian Meatballs

Serve the meatballs in a scooped-out pineapple boat, and you've made your own luau. For a buffet, offer toothpicks to spear the meatballs. For an entrée, serve on a bed of rice.

makes 8 dinner servings or 16 buffet servings

1	medium pineapple
1	pound lean ground beef
½	pound ground pork
½	pound ground veal
1½	cups fresh bread crumbs
2	eggs, whisked until frothy
½	teaspoon marjoram
1	teaspoon dry mustard
	salt and freshly ground black pepper to taste
1	large yellow onion, cut into quarters
2	large red and green bell peppers, seeded and cut into squares
	hot sweet mustard

Cut the pineapple in half lengthwise. Remove the core and discard. Scoop out half of the flesh and measure it out. It should measure somewhere around a cup. Process this by pulsing in the food processor with the steel blade until you have a rough puree. Reserve. Cut the pineapple from the other half into bite-sized chunks and reserve.

Crumble ground meats and add bread crumbs, eggs, and crushed pineapple. Add marjoram, dry mustard, salt, and pepper. Squish with your hands and form into 36 equal-sized meatballs.

Brown the meatballs until cooked through in a large skillet barely filmed with oil. Remove from skillet and reserve. Then, in the pan drippings, brown onions and peppers and stir-fry over medium heat until cooked through.

To serve, toss browned meatballs with pineapple bites, peppers, and onions and scoop into pineapple boats. Serve with toothpicks for spearing. Offer hot sweet mustard on the side for dipping. Or, for an entrée, serve over rice.

Per serving: 458 calories, 23 g. fat, 181 mg. cholesterol, 1,059 mg. sodium

Thai Ground Beef on a Skewer Salad

Having a barbecue in the backyard? Here's a first course that's new, easy, and fun. Grill the skewers of meat over the hibachi, then serve on a bed of ruffled lettuce along with salad vegetables.

makes 6 servings

Meatballs:

1½	pounds lean ground beef
24	wooden skewers, soaked in water

Marinade/Dressing:

¾	cup peanut oil
2	tablespoons sesame oil
⅓	cup rice vinegar
1	tablespoon crushed red pepper
6	cloves garlic, minced
2	jalapeño peppers, seeded and minced
1	tablespoon freshly grated ginger

Salad:

1	head ruffled red-tipped lettuce
1	bunch scallions, white ends cut into brushes
1	piece daikon radish (about 2 inches long), cut into matchstick julienne
1	cup sliced shiitake or button mushrooms
2	medium carrots, peeled and shredded juice of 1 lime

Place the ground beef in a glass dish. Combine marinade/dressing ingredients and pour half of mixture over the beef. Cover and refrigerate both the marinating meat and the remaining salad dressing.

Build a fire in the hibachi. Chill salad plates, then arrange a bed of lettuce topped with onions, radishes, mushrooms, and carrots. Squeeze lime juice over the vegetables and set aside.

Divide the meat into 24 equal parts and form each piece around a wooden skewer, squeezing lightly so the meat sticks. Cook about 2 inches above the white-hot coals, twirling so that the meat cooks evenly and does not burn, no more than 3 to 4 minutes per skewer.

Arrange skewers atop the prepared salads. Pour reserved dressing over all and serve.

Per serving: 567 calories, 46 g. fat, 92 mg. cholesterol, 87 mg. sodium

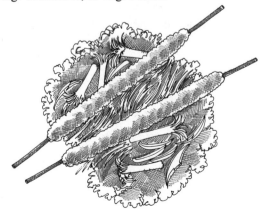

Pot Stickers

At Chinese New Year, families sit around a big table and stuff these dumplings in one of those pleasant communal traditions that makes everyone look forward to the season.

makes 48 pot stickers, serves about 12

Filling:

1	**package fresh spinach**
3	**scallions, finely chopped**
¾	**pound lean ground beef**
1	**knob of ginger, about 1 inch long, peeled and grated**
1	**teaspoon sesame oil**
¼	**teaspoon sugar**
1	**large egg, slightly beaten**
2	**tablespoons low-sodium soy sauce**
1	**teaspoon sherry**
1	**teaspoon orange zest**
¼	**teaspoon hot-pepper sauce**

Sauce:

1	**can (14½ ounces) chicken broth**
⅓	**cup dry sherry**
3	**tablespoons oyster sauce**
1	**tablespoon hoisin sauce**
2	**teaspoons orange zest**
½	**teaspoon hot-pepper sauce**

Wrappers:

1	**package (16 ounces) 3-inch square wonton wrappers**
1	**tablespoon cornstarch dissolved in 2 tablespoons water**
4	**tablespoons peanut oil**

Bring a soup pot of cold water to a boil. Meanwhile, cut the stems from the spinach leaves and thoroughly wash the leaves to remove sand and grit. Drop the leaves into the boiling water and cook for 3 minutes. Pour spinach through a colander and refresh it under cold water. Squeeze excess water from the spinach, then chop finely.

Make the filling by mixing the spinach, scallions, ground beef, ginger, oil, sugar, egg, soy sauce, sherry, orange zest, and hot-pepper sauce. Cover and set aside.

Prepare the sauce by combining the broth, sherry, oyster sauce, hoisin sauce, orange zest, and hot-pepper sauce. Cover and set aside.

Trim the corners from the wonton wrappers, then fill each wrapper with a heaping teaspoon of filling, placed in the center. Moisten the edges of the wrapper with the cornstarch mixture, then fold the wrapper in half, pinching the edges together tightly. Pleat around the edges until you have a small turnover with a flat base and a slightly rounded top. Place each finished dumpling on a piece of waxed paper dusted with cornstarch until you have filled all the dumplings.

Heat 2 tablespoons oil in two 10-inch skillets over medium heat. Cook pot stickers, a few at a time, until the bottoms are golden brown, about 1 minute, then remove and reserve.

Place half of the pot stickers in each skillet, then add half of the sauce, raise the heat to medium-high, cover, and steam for 5 minutes. Uncover and simmer until the sauce evaporates, shaking the pans gently to coat the pot stickers with sauce.

Per serving: 188 calories, 16 g. fat, 71 mg. cholesterol, 333 mg. sodium

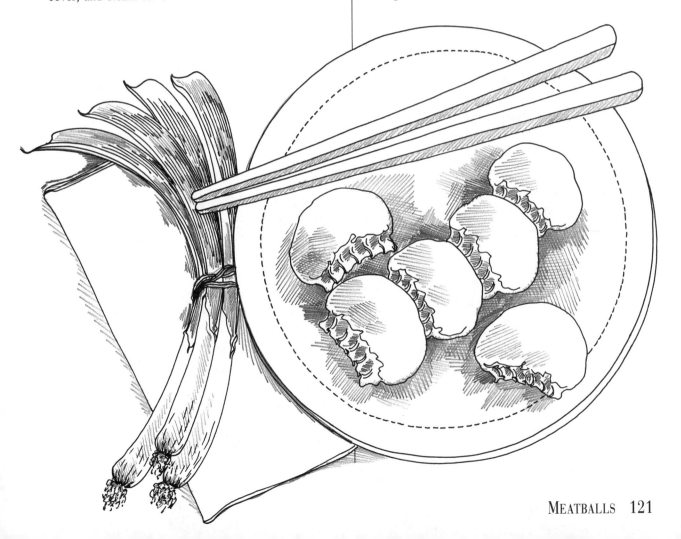

Far East Party Meatballs With Hot Ginger Sauce

Here's a brightly flavored meatball to serve for a wedding reception or big party. You can make and freeze the meatballs and the sauce up to 2 weeks ahead. Served on a glass plate, these meatballs are mouth-wateringly presented on a lettuce leaf with a generous sprinkling of scallions and toasted sesame seeds. You'll need toothpicks or forks to eat them, though, because the sauce is sticky.

makes 100 meatballs, enough for 24 cocktail-sized servings

Meatballs:

3	pounds lean ground beef
3	pounds ground turkey
1	large yellow onion, minced
6	egg whites, whisked
½	cup crushed gingersnaps
4	tablespoons grated fresh ginger
2	tablespoons low-sodium soy sauce

Sauce:

½	cup vegetable oil
½	cup all-purpose flour
1	quart chicken stock
1	cup dry sherry
⅔	cup hoisin sauce
⅔	cup crushed gingersnaps
¾	cup rice vinegar
¼	cup low-sodium soy sauce
½	cup grated fresh ginger
1½	teaspoons red-pepper flakes (or to taste)
	salt and freshly ground black pepper to taste
2	bunches fresh scallions, diagonally cut into thin slices
¾	cup toasted sesame seeds

In a very large bowl, crumble the ground meats. Lightly stir in the onions, then the egg whites. Add gingersnaps, ginger, and soy sauce. Squish it all together with your hands, then form into walnut-sized balls.

Spritz 3 or 4 cookie sheets with nonstick vegetable spray. As you form the meatballs, arrange them in a single layer on the sheets. Cover and refrigerate at least 1 hour. Bake, uncovered, in a 350°F oven, until done, about 20 minutes.

Meanwhile, make the sauce in a large soup pot. Stir oil and flour together over medium heat to make a golden roux. Then pour in stock and sherry and bring to a boil, stirring. Add hoisin sauce, gingersnaps, ½ cup vinegar, soy sauce, ginger, and red-

pepper flakes. Stir to mix. Reduce heat and simmer 30 minutes, stirring from time to time to keep it from sticking to the bottom of the pot.

Taste and adjust seasonings, adding salt, pepper, and remaining vinegar or additional red-pepper flakes, as desired. Add the meatballs to the sauce and let them simmer an additional 30 minutes.

To serve, mound meatballs and sauce in a chafing dish. Sprinkle with scallions and sesame seeds. Alternately, you can serve 2 or 3 meatballs on a butter-head lettuce leaf on a small plate. Pass toothpicks or use forks.

Per serving: 230 calories, 12.4 g. fat, 119 mg. cholesterol, 396 mg. sodium

Party Nacho Meatballs

Using a large, flat tray, create a bed of tortilla chips, top with refried beans and meatballs, then finish with guacamole and fresh lime salsa. Sprigs of cilantro complete this brightly flavored outdoor buffet food.

Make the meatballs bite-sized so your guests can scoop up a meatball, beans, and guacamole on a corn tortilla chip.

makes 16 party servings

Meatballs:
1½	**pounds lean ground beef**
	juice and zest of 1 lime
2	**cloves garlic, pressed**
½	**teaspoon cumin**
1	**jalapeño pepper, seeded and minced**
1	**tablespoon fresh cilantro leaves, minced**

Lime Salsa:
1	**large ripe beefsteak tomato, diced**
2	**large fresh tomatillos, husked and diced**
1	**medium red bell pepper, seeded and diced**
1	**small red onion, diced**
	juice and zest of 1 lime
	salt and pepper to taste
	restaurant-style tortilla chips
2	**cups canned or homemade refried beans**
1	**cup guacamole**
	cilantro sprigs

Crumble ground beef, then add lime juice and zest, garlic, cumin, jalapeños, and cilantro. Squish it all together with your hands, then form into 36 equal-sized meatballs. Brown the meatballs on all sides in a large skillet barely filmed with oil over medium heat until cooked through.

Meanwhile, make the salsa by stirring together the tomatoes, tomatillos, peppers, and onions. Squeeze lime juice over all. Season with salt and pepper and sprinkle lime zest on the top. Cover and refrigerate until serving time.

To assemble, cover the bottom and sides of a large, flat platter with tortilla chips. Heat refried beans in the microwave or in a skillet until bubbly, then spread over the tortillas. Cover with hot meatballs. Add a layer of guacamole and top with lime salsa. Garnish with sprigs of cilantro. Pour more tortilla chips in a basket and set it out alongside the tray so that people can use the tortilla chips to scoop up a bite or a serving.

Per serving: 106 calories, 7 g. fat, 35 mg. cholesterol, 96 mg. sodium

Three-Pepper Meatball Sandwiches

Fill a Kaiser roll with grilled meatballs, three peppers, and mozzarella cheese for a crunchy, bright sandwich.

makes 4 servings

Meatballs:

1	pound lean ground beef
¼	cup fresh bread crumbs
¼	cup milk
½	teaspoon nutmeg
	salt and freshly ground black pepper

Sauce:

3	tablespoons olive oil
2	cloves garlic
1	each medium yellow, red, and green bell pepper, seeded and cut into thin strips
½	teaspoon dried oregano
	salt and freshly ground black pepper to taste
4	slices (about 4 ounces) mozzarella or provolone cheese
4	Kaiser rolls
1	teaspoon red-wine vinegar

Crumble ground beef, then add the bread crumbs, milk, nutmeg, salt, and pepper. Squish it together with your hands and form into 16 meatballs. Brown meatballs on all sides in a large skillet barely filmed with oil over medium heat until cooked through. Reserve in a warmed bowl.

In the same skillet heat 2 tablespoons oil, then sauté garlic with the peppers, oregano, salt, and pepper.

Remove from the heat to a warmed bowl, lay cheese slices over the vegetables, cover, and reserve. Wipe out the skillet and reheat.

Serve sandwiches open-faced by first brushing rolls with the remaining oil, then grilling them in a dry skillet until golden. Sprinkle with vinegar, top each with 4 meatballs and the pepper and cheese mixture.

Per serving: 621 calories, 38 g. fat, 119 mg. cholesterol, 924 mg. sodium

Green Chile Meatballs

Serve these meatballs in a shredded lettuce nest atop a flour tortilla you've deep-fried and formed into a basket. Top with grated cheddar, a dollop of sour cream, scallion rings, and a black olive. You can make all this ahead and assemble it at the last minute. The flour tortilla nest can be cold, the lettuce should be, and the meatballs and sauce should be bubbly hot. It makes a nice hot and cold salad in one serving.

makes 6 servings

Meatballs:

1	pound lean ground beef
1	can (4 ounces) diced green chilies, drained
	salt and red and black peppers to taste
1	egg white, whisked until foamy
½	cup fresh bread crumbs

Sauce:

1	can (8 ounces) tomato sauce
½	teaspoon Tabasco sauce
1	teaspoon molasses
1	tablespoon cider vinegar
1	tablespoon fresh grated ginger
4	cloves garlic, pressed
½	can of beer
	salt and freshly ground black pepper to taste

6	large flour tortillas
½	head iceberg lettuce, shredded
1	cup shredded Longhorn cheese
4	tablespoons sour cream
3	scallions and tops, cut into thin rings
6	large black olives, pitted

Crumble the ground beef, then mix with chilies, salt, and peppers. Pour over the egg whites and bread crumbs, then squish it all together with your hands. Form into 24 equal-sized meatballs.

Brown the meatballs on all sides in a large skillet lightly filmed with oil over medium heat until cooked through.

Meanwhile make the sauce. In a large saucepan, mix the tomato sauce, Tabasco sauce, molasses, vinegar, ginger, garlic, beer, salt, and pepper. Bring to a boil, then simmer over low heat until thick and the flavors are well married.

As the meatballs are browned, transfer them to the sauce and let them simmer 10 to 15 minutes longer.

To assemble, fry a flour tortilla in deep fat until beginning to brown, then quickly flip it out over a bowl so that it will cool in the shape of a bowl. Fill the bottom with lettuce. Add a layer of meatballs and sauce. Top with cheese, sour cream, onions, and an olive. Serve at once.

Per serving: 588 calories, 28 g. fat, 144 mg. cholesterol, 724 mg. sodium

Amish Yumasetta Meatballs

Make a pan of egg noodles, slice some red ripe tomatoes, and dinner's done.

makes 4 servings

Meatballs:

1	pound lean ground beef
½	teaspoon brown sugar
	freshly ground black pepper to taste
¼	cup finely minced onions
¼	cup finely minced fresh parsley
	parsley sprigs

Sauce:

1	can (14½ ounces) tomato soup
1	can (14½ ounces) cream of chicken soup
1	package (16 ounces) wide egg noodles
½	cup shredded colby cheese

Crumble the ground beef, then add brown sugar and pepper. Squish in onions and minced parsley until well mixed. Form into 16 equal-sized meatballs, then brown in a large skillet barely filmed with oil over medium heat until cooked through.

To make the sauce, add the soups to the skillet. Cover and simmer about 20 minutes.

Meanwhile, cook the noodles following the package directions.

To serve, drain the noodles, place them in a wide, flat serving platter, then mound meatballs and sauce on top. Sprinkle with cheese and garnish with parsley sprigs.

Per serving: 639 calories, 29 g. fat, 129 mg. cholesterol, 747 mg. sodium

Spicy Meatballs

Make a pot of rice and toss a salad. You'll want lots of iced tea to cool the fires. It's that good.

makes 4 servings

Meatballs:
1	**pound lean ground beef**
1	**medium onion, diced**
1	**jalapeño pepper (or to taste), seeded and diced**
1	**cup soft bread crumbs**
2	**egg whites, whisked until foamy**
	salt and freshly ground black pepper to taste

Sauce:
1	**cup bottled barbecue sauce**
1	**teaspoon Worcestershire sauce**
½	**teaspoon dry mustard**
1	**teaspoon brown sugar**
2	**cloves garlic, pressed**
	salt and freshly ground black pepper

Crumble ground beef, then add onions, jalapeños, bread crumbs, egg whites, salt, and pepper. Squish it together with your hands, then form into 16 equal-sized meatballs. Brown the meatballs on all sides in a large skillet barely filmed with oil over medium heat until cooked through.

Meanwhile, make the sauce. Stir together the barbecue sauce, Worcestershire sauce, mustard, brown sugar, and garlic. Taste and adjust seasonings with salt and pepper. Pour over the meatballs, cover, and simmer 10 minutes. Serve over cooked rice.

Per serving: 486 calories, 19 g. fat, 92 mg. cholesterol, 2,686 mg. sodium

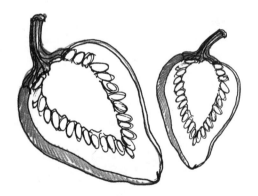

Apple-Onion Meatballs

Here's a fix-it-and-forget-it suppertime dish. Form the meatballs, pour sauce over them, and bake. Make a pan of rice, and you get a succulent one-dish dinner you'll want to make again and again.

makes 4 servings

Meatballs:

1	**pound lean ground beef**
¾	**cup applesauce**
½	**cup chopped onions**
¾	**cup fresh bread crumbs**
1	**egg white, whisked**
	salt and freshly ground black pepper to taste

Sauce:

1	**can (8 ounces) tomato sauce**
2	**teaspoons prepared mustard**
1	**tablespoon Worcestershire sauce**
1	**medium carrot, peeled and grated**
1	**medium onion, minced**
1	**rib celery, minced**
½	**bell pepper, seeded and finely chopped**
	salt and freshly ground black pepper to taste

Preheat the oven to 350°F. Crumble ground beef, then stir in the applesauce, onions, bread crumbs, egg white, salt, and pepper. Squish it with your hands, then form into 16 equal-sized balls. Place the meatballs in a 3-quart casserole dish.

Make the sauce, stirring together the tomato sauce, mustard, Worcestershire sauce, carrots, onions, celery, and peppers. Taste and adjust seasonings with salt and pepper.

Pour the sauce over the meatballs, then pop them into the oven and bake for 1 hour. Serve meatballs and sauce over rice.

Per serving: 462 calories, 20 g. fat, 160 mg. cholesterol, 1,573 mg. sodium

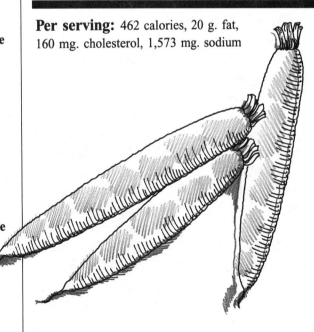

Jarlsberg Meatball Puffs

Here's an addition to the buffet table that is made easy by using commercially prepared frozen puff pastry. Inside each puff pastry pocket is a miniature meatball and a melting bite of Jarlsberg Swiss cheese.

makes 24 3-inch triangular puffs

½	**pound lean ground beef**
½	**pound fully cooked ham, diced**
1	**medium onion, diced**
2	**tablespoons finely chopped parsley**
	salt and freshly ground black pepper to taste
1	**pound frozen puff pastry**
1	**cup shredded Jarlsberg cheese**
2	**tablespoons toasted sesame seeds**
2	**egg whites, whisked**

Preheat the oven to 375°F. Crumble ground beef, then add ham, onions, and parsley. Season to taste with salt and pepper. Form into 24 equal-sized meatballs and refrigerate.

Meanwhile, thaw puff pastry according to package directions. Then, on a lightly floured board, roll each sheet of pastry into a 10½ x 14-inch oblong piece. Cut each of the 2 sheets into 12 equal 3½-inch squares.

Place a meatball on each pastry square. Top with a generous pinch of cheese and sprinkling of sesame seeds. Fold the pastry square in half, making a triangle. Pinch the edges shut with the tines of a fork and place on an ungreased cookie sheet. Once you have all the puffs made, brush the tops with egg white and sprinkle with additional sesame seeds.

Bake in the oven until the pastry is golden and meatballs are cooked, about 25 minutes.

Per serving: 167 calories, 11 g. fat, 35 mg. cholesterol, 203 mg. sodium

Meatball Stroganoff

Here's a lightened version of an old favorite. Use light sour cream and lean ground beef and you will have shaved off unwanted fats and cholesterol. Serve on a bed of egg noodles and garnish with sprigs of parsley.

Remember, cracker meal is easily made by whirring saltine crackers in the food processor or blender until they're pulverized. Of course, you can buy it if you want to.

makes 6 servings

Meatballs:

1½	pounds lean ground beef
1	medium yellow onion, minced
¼	cup cracker meal
¼	cup low-fat (2%) milk
2	cloves garlic, pressed
	salt and freshly ground black pepper to taste

Sauce:

¼	cup all-purpose flour
1	cup light sour cream or plain nonfat yogurt
1	can (10½ ounces) beef broth
3	tablespoons tomato paste
1	teaspoon Worcestershire sauce
	salt and freshly ground black pepper to taste
1	package (16 ounces) wide egg noddles
½	cup finely chopped parsley

Crumble ground beef, then add onions, cracker meal, milk, garlic, salt, and pepper. Squish it all together with your hands and form into 36 equal-sized balls. Brown the meatballs in a large skillet barely filmed with oil over medium heat until cooked through, then set them aside.

Meanwhile, make the sauce. Stir flour into the sour cream or yogurt, making a lump-free mixture. Heat broth in the skillet with tomato paste and Worcestershire sauce until it boils. Stir in the sour cream or yogurt mixture and heat to boiling. Taste and adjust seasoning with salt and pepper. Add meatballs and simmer for 10 minutes or so before serving. Meanwhile, cook noodles according to package directions. Serve on a bed of egg noodles and sprinkle with parsley.

Per serving: 432 calories, 20 g. fat, 96 mg. cholesterol, 661 mg. sodium

Super Meatball Casserole

Make this dish in less than 30 minutes for a fast and fancy meatball dinner. All you need to accompany it is a bitter lettuce salad and a loaf of crusty French bread.

makes 8 servings

Meatballs:

½   pound lean ground beef
½   pound ground pork
½   cup fresh bread crumbs
½   cup grated Parmesan cheese
2   egg whites, whisked until foamy
¼   teaspoon freshly grated nutmeg
⅛   teaspoon ground cumin
1   clove garlic, pressed
1   tablespoon parsley, finely cut with scissors
     salt and freshly ground black pepper to taste
2   tablespoons olive oil

Sauce:

1   can (16 ounces) tomatoes (with juice)
½   teaspoon sugar
1   teaspoon dried rosemary
½   cup dry red wine
1   bay leaf
1   tablespoon chopped fresh basil or parsley
     salt and freshly ground black pepper

Ingredients for Casserole:

4   sweet or hot Italian sausages (about 1 pound)
1   medium yellow onion, finely chopped
½   pound brown mushrooms, thinly sliced
1   large yellow or red bell pepper, seeded and sliced
½   cup freshly grated Parmesan cheese

Crumble the ground meats, then add the bread crumbs, Parmesan, egg whites, nutmeg, cumin, garlic, parsley, salt, and pepper. Squish it all together with your hands and form into 36 walnut-sized meatballs. Set aside in the refrigerator.

Meanwhile, begin simmering the sauce in a medium pan. Mix tomatoes and juice, sugar, rosemary, wine, bay leaf, and basil or parsley. Simmer about 10 minutes. Taste and adjust seasonings with salt and pepper.

Using a 12-inch skillet, brown the sausages over medium-high heat, pricking them to allow the juices to run into the pan. Cook along with the onions, mushrooms, and peppers. Transfer to a flame-proof casserole dish. Brown the meatballs in the same skillet with oil, then add them to the casserole.

Ladle a little sauce into the skillet to deglaze the pan, then pour all the sauce over the meats, cover, and simmer about 10 minutes. (Alternately you can put this in a 350°F oven for 25 minutes). Let the dish stand 10 minutes and discard bay leaf before serving.

Meanwhile, cook up a pound of your favorite pasta and serve this casserole on a dinner plate with a side of penne tossed with fresh basil or linguini tossed with Italian parsley. Top with generous servings of Parmesan.

Per serving: 655 calories, 50 g. fat, 89 mg. cholesterol, 1,385 mg. sodium

Jalapeño Deviled Meatball Sandwich

Hot as the devil, welcome as heaven.

makes 4 servings

Meatballs:

1   pound lean ground beef
1   large jalapeño pepper, seeded and minced
1   cup fresh bread crumbs
¼   cup milk
     salt and freshly ground black pepper to taste

Cheese Sauce:

¼   cup shredded mozzarella or string cheese
¼   cup chopped roasted red pepper (from a jar)
2   tablespoons finely chopped fresh parsley

Sandwich Makings:

4   large flour tortillas
4   red-tipped lettuce leaves
¼   cup sour cream or plain nonfat yogurt
     cilantro sprigs
     lime slices
     jalapeño shards

Crumble the ground beef, and sprinkle with 1 tablespoon minced jalapeños. Add bread crumbs and milk. Season with salt and pepper. Squish it all together with your hands and form into 24 walnut-sized meatballs.

Brown the meatballs in a hot skillet barely filmed with oil over medium heat until cooked through.

Meanwhile, make the sauce. Mix cheese, red peppers, remaining minced jalapeños, and parsley. Transfer meatballs to the cheese mixture.

To serve, heat the tortillas, covered, in the microwave, 20 seconds at 100 percent (HIGH), then tuck a piece of lettuce into the tortilla, add a spoonful of sour cream or yogurt, and top with a serving of meatballs and cheese. Garnish with cilantro, limes, and jalapeños.

Per serving: 626 calories, 27 g. fat, 113 mg. cholesterol, 1,507 mg. sodium

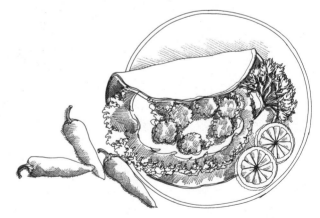

Afterword

THE ABSOLUTE TOP: AMERICA'S BEST-LOVED HAMBURGER

By the time I'd cooked and tasted 100 recipes to complete this collection, I knew I wanted to offer to you the very best hamburger I could find.

To that end, I ran a contest in my weekly newspaper column asking readers to tell me about their favorite hamburger. The response was overwhelming. I about decided that if you think America is apple pie, forget it. America is the hamburger.

From Florida to Washington, from Maine to California, Americans everywhere equate their fondest memories of adolescence with the all-American hamburger, drive-ins, french fries, and an assortment of special drinks. Not to mention boyfriends, fathers, and love—that wonderful moment of awakening that marks adolescence for all. The hamburger—aromatic, hot, handsome, and mouth-watering—was there for us all.

Here's what some of the readers said:

"Everyone's great American hamburger is more than just a patty and a sesame seed bun.

That special never-to-be-forgotten taste you long for is actually a time, a place, and a revered memory that is yours alone."

"The promise of going into town to get a hamburger made working out in the fields all day a lot more bearable . . . For 30 cents you got a hamburger with mustard and a lot of onions . . . ."

"It is fun to imagine the taste, smell, and feel of my favorite burger, because while doing so, for ever so short a time, I am 18 again, with no worries, endless friends, and a future full of anything I want to do or be."

One reader noted that a hamburger in high school was a social affair. They'd ride to Bill's Drive-In in a borrowed Hudson and order a burger and fries. The girls would flirt with the boys in neighboring cars while downing their burgers.

Another reader remembered hamburgers on Saturday night. Her dad would take her to see a double-feature Western movie at the best movie house in town, then, afterward, driving back home, they'd stop for a hamburger at a neighborhood café.

Our reader remembers that she had a crush on the cook and that she always ordered a chocolate malt on the side. When that good-looking cook slapped the patty on the grill and looked

into her eyes and asked "onions?" she'd look back at him and answer simply, "everything."

Fathers seem to play a prominent role in many people's memories of hamburgers. One reader wrote that her father owned a café, and he taught her to make hamburgers. From the time she was big enough to stand on a wooden box to reach the black iron griddle on the stove, she made hamburgers.

Her dad sold the burgers for ten cents and soda pop for a nickel. For ten cents he'd give you a glass of fresh apple or cherry cider dipped from a wooden keg.

If a customer asked for cheese, it was a nickel extra. If people asked for tomatoes and lettuce, her dad would say in a disgusted voice, "You don't want a hamburger, you want a vegetable burger."

One reader reported that during her eight-year stint as a vegetarian, the only meat she ever craved was hamburger. The first thing she ordered when she left her vegetarian ways was—you guessed it—a hamburger.

She first ate hamburgers at the Tick Tock Drive-In in Portland, Oregon, in the thirties.

These hamburgers were made from very lean meat, with oversized buns, shredded lettuce, and a secret sauce (some mixture of catsup and mayo with chopped onions and pickle). The hamburger was so juicy it was served in an oval-shaped, flat-bottomed aluminum "pocket" to catch the drips.

Later in the forties, after she and her family had moved to Darien, Connecticut, she ate hamburgers at a teenager haunt called Bob's, built in an old railroad car. The teenagers mobbed the counter, never considering "take-out," and stood shoulder to shoulder in the old railroad car, eating and mingling.

Bob made hamburgers on his big grill by first slapping a huge lump of real butter on the grill. Then onto that went extra-lean hamburger patties. Then another swipe of butter was put on the hot patty along with a big dollop of Bob's homemade mayonnaise and a thin wedge of lettuce. Never tomatoes or pickles. And all for 15 cents.

Distilling these recipes, and trying them all, here's what we vote for as number one.

Eckhardt's Hopped-Up Hamburger

We serve our favorite hamburger on our own toasted home-style buns or English muffins, along with mustard and mayonnaise, frilly lettuce, thick slabs of home-grown tomatoes, slivers of purple onion, and thinly sliced sweet bread-and-butter pickles.

makes 4 servings

1	**pound lean ground beef**
⅛	**teaspoon cayenne pepper**
½	**teaspoon freshly ground black pepper**
4	**cloves garlic, pressed**
2	**tablespoons grated yellow onions**
1	**teaspoon Worcestershire sauce**
1	**tablespoon hot prepared mustard**
	salt

Squish all the ingredients together, except the salt, with your hands, then form into 4 slightly rounded patties. Cover and refrigerate.

Preheat the charcoal or gas grill. Grill the burgers until done, turning only once. Salt the burgers only after they've been turned. During the last few moments, place the buns face-down on the grill to toast. Then serve the burgers on hot buns to your guests and let them dress the burgers as they choose.

Per serving: 350 calories, 12 g. fat, 103 mg. cholesterol, 188 mg. sodium

NOTES

NOTES

KITCHEN METRICS

For cooking and baking convenience, the Metric Commission of Canada suggests the following for adapting to metric measurement. The table gives approximate, rather than exact, conversions.

SPOONS

¼ teaspoon	= 1 milliliter
½ teaspoon	= 2 milliliters
1 teaspoon	= 5 milliliters
1 tablespoon	= 15 milliliters
2 tablespoons	= 25 milliliters
3 tablespoons	= 50 milliliters

CUPS

¼ cup	= 50 milliliters
⅓ cup	= 75 milliliters
½ cup	= 125 milliliters
⅔ cup	= 150 milliliters
¾ cup	= 175 milliliters
1 cup	= 250 milliliters

OVEN TEMPERATURES

200°F	= 100°C
225°F	= 110°C
250°F	= 120°C
275°F	= 140°C
300°F	= 150°C
325°F	= 160°C
350°F	= 180°C
375°F	= 190°C
400°F	= 200°C
425°F	= 220°C
450°F	= 230°C
475°F	= 240°C

INDEX

ABOUT THE AUTHOR

Linda West Eckhardt is the author of eight cookbooks including *The Only Texas Cookbook, Barbecue Indoors and Out,* and *Bread in Half the Time,* winner of the 1990 International Association of Culinary Professionals Award for Best Cookbook of the Year.

She also writes weekly newspaper columns for *The Oregonian* and for *The Medford Mail Tribune.* In addition, she has published more than 100 magazine articles, a dozen short stories in literary journals, and has fiction included in the anthologies *South by Southwest* and *A Texas Christmas.* She has edited cookbooks and a literary anthology and teaches writing and cooking. Her works in progress include another cookbook and a novel.

Eckhardt lives in Ashland, Oregon, with her psychiatrist husband, Joe, two dogs, and two cats. Between them they have six grown children.